GLEANINGS FROM INDIAN CLASSICS

GLEANINGS

FROM

INDIAN CLASSICS

EDITED BY

MANMATHA NATH DUTT, M. A.

GYAN

Published by

GYAN

Gyan Publishing House
5, Ansari Road
Daryaganj, New Delhi-110002
Phone: 011-47034999, 9811692060
E-mail: books@gyanbooks.com

Distribution Network
gyanbooks.com
India, USA, Canada, UK, Australia, France

ISBN: 978-81-212-8690-9 (PB)
First Published, 1893

2nd Impression 2023

Printed at: Gyan Press, Delhi.

GLEANINGS FROM INDIAN CLASSICS
Editor: Manmatha Nath Dutt

CLEANINGS FROM INDIAN CLASSICS.

"What mortal now can harm,
Or foemen vex us more
Through thee, beyond alarm
Immortal God, we soar."

GLEANINGS

FROM

INDIAN CLASSICS.

EDITED BY

MANMATHA NATH DUTT, M, A.,

Rector, Keshub Academy,

Editor of the English Translation of the Ramayana, Srimadbhagabatam and Vishnupuranam.

CALCUTTA:

AT THE DEVA PRESS.

1893.

INTRODUCTION.

The Hindus and their Religion are the most misunderstood thing in the modern world. The civilized people of the Western World labour under the notion that the Hindus are a people a little better than the aborigines of Africa and their Religion is no better than the grossest sort of idolatry. The fault does not lie with them. The Hindus are by nature very retiring and modest; they never thrust themselves upon others,—especially to nations who are in every way different from them. A foreigner, if he passes all his life in India, will never know the autonomy of a Hindu-home; he will never know their domestic arrangements,—he will never understand what sort of being a Hindu really is; for a Hindu is too bashful and too modest to defend himself by explaining his religion and morals or manners and customs. They cannot be easily known from their books, for they are written in a language very difficult to master. Thus the popular notion of the Western World is, that the Hindus are semi-aborigines, who worship woods and stones.

But a few of the great scholars of Europe and America have a different notion of the Hindus. This has been done by their study of the Sanskrit language. They have found in it a mine of wealth, —they have found a literature, adorned with the best grace and diction, with the highest poetry and rhetoric, —a philosophy with thoughts too high and too comprehensive to grasp,—a religion beautiful in conception, grand in perception and sublime in its execution. But alas, they are too few to remove the notion that is held by Europe from the day when two branches of the same Aryan stock met after years of seperation in the plains of India! They have spoken on public platforms, they have lectured in class-rooms, they have written in the papers, they have published books and translated Sanskrit works, but their works are too high for the popular mind; the learned and the scholars only have found that Hindus and their Religion are not what they were led to believe.

This book is an attempt to popularize the noble work begun by Sir William Jones and Colebrooke, and is being carried on by Monier Williams, Maxmuller and a host of other great men. The Hindus live in their religion; there is nothing in his every day life which is not co-mixed with his religion; one cannot study them without studying his literature, philosophy and religion. But all these are locked up n a language difficult to master and hence the works published by the great orientalists have failed to influence the popular mind.

The Hindu Philosophy is too high a subject for an ordinary intellect to get at; the Hindu religion is based on a Theology too complicated to be easily grasped; but still the religion has a great hold over the popular mind, and has extended its influence to every stratum of the society, which we do not find any where else.

The only means, by which the present false notion regarding the Hindus and their Religion can be removed, is to popularize their Literature, Philosophy and Religion amongst the Western nations. The great Hindu *Rishis* adopted this very means to extend the influence of their religion; they popularized their Religion and Philosophy in such a way as to send it to the innermost recess of a Hindu home. They did it by writing innumerable *Puránas*. Now these *Puránas* are religious books, in which Philosophy and Theology have been told in interesting tales, in which religion has been preached through popular annals, legends and histories, in which the the crudest metaphysical points have been explained in plain, sweet and popular verses. These tales, these annals, legends and histories, these sweet and and popular verses were read by thousands, were heard by millions when sung by village ministrels, and were told by every old matron and heard by all children. Thus they became, and with them the Hindu Philosophy and Religion, the household property and heritage of every Hindu, man, woman or child. They raised them to a very high standard of civilization—a civilization which two thousand years' continual foreign struggles of every sort,—physical, moral, social, political and religious, —could not destroy. They instilled into their society moral virtues which nowhere are to be found ; they made the Hindu homes the sweetest and the happiest in all the world.

We do not exaggerate ; so long we cannot remove the notion that is predominant all over the Western World, we know we shall find none to agree with us in saying what we have just now said. This work is an attempt in that direction. This is an attempt to popularize the Hindu Literature, Philosophy and religion amongst the Western nations. We are treading the footsteps of the great *Rishis*. We are following the examples and adopting the means of those great men, who made India what it is. We shall give their tales, their annals, legends and histories, their sweet verses and sweeter poems in popular and easy English, suiting modern tastes and Western methods. Hindu Literature, History, Philosophy and Religion are so extensive that it is not expected to be mastered in a day or explained in a book. This little work is the first step to give an idea of them,—it will be followed by a series of works, in each and every one of which attempts will be made to popularize Hindu Literature, History Philosophy and Religion.

To

His Highness

Sir Veeracarala Vurma

Knight Commander of the most Eminent

Order of the Indian Empire,

Maharaja of Cochin.

This Little Book is Respectfully Dedicated

as a Token of Gratitude by the

Editor.

CONTENTS.

PAGE

Battle of Gods and Demons . . . . . . 1.

Shiva and Sati . . . . 19.

Srikrishna . . . . 30.

The Monkey War . . . . 57.

The Battle of Kurukshetra . . . . . . 79.

Nala and Damayanti . . . . 105.

Sribatsa and Chinta . . . . 115.

Prahlada . . . . 126.

The Lost Ring . . . . 135.

The Boy Devotee . . . . 150.

Sabitri and Satyavan . . . . 156.

Debjani . . . . 165.

Bilwamangala . . . . 176.

Harishchandra . . . . 183.

Parasurama . . . . 196.

Bishaya . . . . 201.

The Danava King . . . . 209.

TALES OF IND.

BATTLE OF GODS AND DEMONS.

THE great *Trinity* manifested itself in three forms, namely, *Brahmá*, the Creator, *Vishnu*, the Preserver, and *Shiva*, the Destroyer. The universe was created by the first and was filled with innumerable *forces*; but they were of two classes,—positive and negative,—the preserving and the destroying *forces*. One class was engaged in preserving the universe, the other was always for its destruction. The preserving forces, such as the air, fire, water, were the embodiments of all that was good,—the others were quite the reverse. The former were called the *Devas*, or the Gods, the latter were called the *Dánavas* or the Demons. *Vishnu* was the Great Protector of the gods, and *Shiva* was that of the demons. The former had his seat in *Baikuntha*, and his almighty power (omnipotence) was his wife, and she was called *Lakshmi*. *Shiva* lived in *Kailásh*, and his wife was *Durgá*.*

---

* Readers are to understand that the names *Vishnu* and *Shiva* are the mere names of the two great Spirits of God. *Lakshmi* and *Durgá* are also the mere names of His preserving and destroying forces, and are not distinct beings. The gods and the demons are the created *elements*. The tale of the battle of gods and demons is an allegorical account of the ever-lasting struggle of the elements, the struggle of Life and Death, the struggle of the *forces* of preservation and destruction, the battle of the good and the evil, that is continuing from the beginning of time. The tale is to be found in the books of every religion, but told in various ways. The Christians have Satan, a quite distinct being from God; but the Hindus say that He as *Vishnu* is *All-good* and He as *Shiva* is *All-evil*. He has created the gods as well as the demons, and they are both protected, loved and preserved by Him;—and they stand as brothers in relation. In this tale all these forces have been personified and made to live and act as human beings, as required in an allegory. The readers should know that the Hindu *Rishis* had said that the good elements, both material and spiritual, are immortal and none of them could ever be destroyed; whereas the demons, *i.e.* the evil elements, are both material and spiritual; but though they are never exterminated, yet some of them are always destroyed. They should also mark that the demons were the greatest favourites of *God* as *Shiva*; but He Himself destroyed them by His destructive and omnipotent force, which had been named *Durgá*, His wife, when required to keep equillibrium in

Vishnu wanted to make his favourites,namely the gods, immortal and powerful. *Vishnu*, being the Preserver, naturally wants to preserve the gods ;—to preserve means to bestow immortality. He asked the gods to churn* the great ocean,† so that ambrosia might be produced. The demons offered their services to the gods, which they could not decline. Thus both the gods and the demons laboured incessantly for years, till the ocean gave forth the wonderful liquid.‡ Then there arose a great disagreement between the gods and the demons; —both parties wanting to take possession of it. *Vishnu* appeared before them as a most beautiful damsel§ and offered to divide and distribute it amongst the gods and the demons. They were all charmed with her exquisite beauty and they agreed to submit to her will.

the universe. But both the gods and the demons exist and fight for supremacy till the end of time. Thus *Brahmá* is the infinite base from which elements have evolved ; *Vishnu* preserves them, *Shiva* destroys them ; out of this grand struggle Nature with her beauty, sublimity and laws has been formed. This tale tries to explain this grand philosophy of the Hindus.

* The churning of the ocean means the actions of the contrary forces, the effect of which is this beautiful universe. Readers are well aware that the effects of the so many contrary forces of gravitation are the orders and regularities in the starry universe.

† Evidently the ocean means the original chaotic state of the universe.—Milton's sea of Chaos.

‡ This ambrosia is the immortality of Nature.

§ This damsel is Nature ; she always rules over the elements.

She told them that as the gods were the elder brothers of the demons, they should be served first. The demons acquiesced; and she began to distribute the immortalising liquid amongst the gods. Soon she gave away almost the whole of the quantity, and herself drank the rest. The demons were exasperated; they rushed upon her in all fury, but the gods soon came to her help. There were great fightings,—but as the gods had become immortal and powerful by drinking the ambrosial wine, the demons were soon defeated and routed.

Their Protector and God, the terrible *Shiva*, came to their assistance. He asked them to churn the ocean again. But alas, instead of ambrosia the ocean vomitted forth deadly poison.*

The quarrel that was bred on the shores of the churned ocean continued for thousands of years; the battle that began between gods and demons continued to eternity.

The demons were very powerful and some of them became invincible and unconquerable by the grace of their god *Shiva*. Though they could not exterminate the gods, yet often they defeated them, drove them from heaven and took possession of the celestial regions.

* This poison means Death; *i. e.* the force of destruction. *Shiva* the God can give only destruction and death.

There were great wars and terrible battles between the gods and the demons. Sometimes the former were defeated, sometimes the latter. We shall narrate only the greatest of these wars and battles.*

[2]

THERE were supposed to be thirty three millions of gods and goddesses,—but *Indra* was their King and Lord. After the defeat of the *Dánavas* on the shore of the churned ocean, the gods lived in peace and happiness for many long years, till a great *Dánava* was born, who was known by the name of *Bitrásura.* Under him the demons gradually gained strength, for he was a great warrior and a great general. He collected round him all the demons who had been scattered over the universe after their defeat at the battle for ambrosia; he formed them into a great army, filled them with hopes of success and promised them victory with the possession of heaven and its happiness.

* There are a good many tales, in which we find the demons born as human beings; they bred sin and vice and oppressed humanity. The gods had to come down and assume human shapes to check and destroy them. The *Rámáyana* is an instance. *Rávana* and his *Rákshasas* were the demons, and *Ráma* was *Vishnu* and the monkeys were the gods. But in this tale we shall narrate only three wars, in which they fought in their own shapes and not as human beings.

Under him they rose in rebellion and declared war with the gods; under him they marched and encamped at the gates of heaven. They could never forgive the gods—their eternal enemies; they determined to gain heaven or to die in the field of battle.

The war went on for years; there were many sanguinary battles and hot skirmishes; innumerable demons were killed and wounded, but the gods could not drive them from heaven. They grew weakened and crippled by continual wars. They lost heart and thought of flying from their happy heaven. *Indra* became anxious and went to *Brahmá* for advice and help. "My dear son," said the Creator, "Go to the great *Dadhichi*.* Ask for his bones; make a thunder out of them; for without thunder ye would not be able to kill *Bitra* and to drive away his demonaic hordes from the gates of heaven."

The king of the gods hastened to the great *Rishi Dadhichi*, and narrated to him all the evil deeds of the wicked demons, their attacks on heaven and their oppressions all over the universe. "Venerable father," prayed the heavenly king, "If thou dost not save us and with us the universe, we have no other hope of safety." "My dear son," said *Dadhichi*, "Tell me what I can do for thee." Indra told him all that had been said to him by the great Creator. He told him that he had come to

* He was a great *Rishi*.

him to pray for his bones. "Is this all?" said *Dadhichi*, "I shall gladly give my life for the good of the world."

He then renounced his life and *Indra* hastened back to heaven with his bones. There was great joy amongst the gods and they cheered again and again, when their king appeared amongst them with the much-desired bones.

Soon the dreadful thunder was created and every arrangement was made to attack the demons. A great battle was fought in the fields of heaven; there was hard fighting on both sides, till the terrible thunder was let loose. It soon crushed the demon-king into atoms and hurled his vast army down from the ethereal height. They fell from the height of heaven to the very depths of the infernal regions, there to lie insensible for many a long year.*

[3]

AFTER the fall of the demons from the heaven's height, the gods lived for many years very happily and in peace, the demons never venturing to attack them. Their power had been thoroughly broken down and they had neither the heart nor the courage to venture out of the infernal regions and to call the gods to battle.

* Readers should notice the similarity of this battle with that of Satan with the gods in the fields of heaven. Evidently either of the two must have been borrowed from the other.

But they were not at rest ; many of them issued forth in disguise and tried to disturb the gods in various ways. Sometimes they would come stealthily near the gates of heaven and look wistfully on its beauty and happiness ; the boldest of them only would pass into the celestial kingdom. He would steal the wealth of heaven ; he would disturb the peace of heavenly homes and return to tell his less bold compeers of his wonderful deeds of courage and adventure. These wicked and bold demons would often steal the celestial damsels and carry them down to the infernal regions ; they would often steal heavenly children and make them their eternal slaves.

Thus many years rolled on ;—the gods, though disturbed,did not think it proper to declare another war with the demons ; but at last a *Dánava*, named *Shoma*, stole the beautiful wife of *Brihashpati*, the great Preceptor of the gods. The wicked *Dánava* tempted her to the path of sin ; she fell ; and she was enticed away to the kingdom of darkness.

The old Preceptor grew wild with grief and anger ; he hastened to *Indra* and appealed to him to rescue his beloved wife from the clutches of the demons. His words were mandates to the gods ; they all felt injured and insulted by the gross injury done to their great leader.

So the order was passed ; king *Indra* called his generals to arms and his gods to rally round him, for another mortal struggle with their eternal enemies. Every arrangement was made and they marched out from heaven to chastise the demons and rescue the stolen goddess.

The demons resolved to stand firm ; they determined to have another great struggle with the gods, whatever might be the final result. They elected a great *Dánava*, named *Táraká*, as their king and leader; they made every preparation to give their enemies a hot reception.

Their choice of a leader was the best possible. The great *Dánava, Tárakásura*, was really invincible in arms and unequalled in statecraft. For many a long year he had been praying to the God, *Shiva*, and had at last got his blessings, thereby becoming invincible to thunder and to all heavenly weapons.

The gods and the demons met,—met after a long period,—like two wild whirlpools in a great storm. The war continued for years, both parties fighting, as only the gods and the demons could fight. Again and again the thunder was let loose, but to no purpose ; the demons gradually gained ground. The celestial army was daily broken down and the gods were at last defeated and routed. They fled in hot haste towards heaven, pursued by the successful and elated demons.

They fled precipitously into their kingdom and shut up its gates; but alas, fortune was against them! The demons stormed their heavenly citadel, drove them out of their celestial homes, and took possession of the much-desired kingdom. The gods fled in all directions and were scattered over the universe. At last heaven was lost.

Indra, king of the gods, having been defeated and driven out of his kingdom, went to the Creator for advice and help. "My son," said he, "Do not be disheartened; such is the will of Providence. *Shiva* is immersed in great *Yoga** on the death of his wife;† and this is the reason of the demons becoming unconquerable. Go to *Vishnu* and he will advise thee as to what to do in order to regain thy Paradise."

Indra went to *Baikuntha* and prayed to its Lord for help. He narrated all that had happened and told him the miserable plight into which the gods and the goddesses had fallen. "My beloved son," said the great God, "I have no power to destroy; I can preserve and I have preserved you from death by bestowing upon you immortality. None can destroy the demons except *Shiva*. His wife is born as a daughter of king *Himálaya*. Go and try to get her married with the Great Destroyer. The son that

* Read the particulars of *Yoga* in the Appendix.

† Read the particulars of the death in the Tale *Shiva* and *Sati*.

would be born of this marriage, would regain heaven for you."

The king of the gods returned to his hiding-place. There held he a confidential council with his ministers and generals; it was settled to despatch *Nárada** to king *Himálaya* with the proposal of the marriage. But the difficulty was not there;—the gods knew not what to do to rouse up *Shiva* from his *Yoga*-sleep. "Oh, king," suggested one, "Take *Madan*† with you. There is none in the universe who can withstand the arrows of Love. Surely *Shiva's Yoga* would be broken and *Nárada* would be able to propose to him the marriage."

The suggestion was adopted and every arrangement was made. The chief gods went towards *Kailása*, and *Nárada* promised to join them there, after securing the consent of king *Himálaya*.

On the heights of the hoary *Kailása* sat *Shiva* in his great *Yoga*-sleep. Calmness reigned all over the place, the sway of solitude having extended far and wide. Not a sound, not the least noise, could venture to disturb the peace of the awful place; the wind had ceased to breathe where the great Destroyer sat in his majesty.

The gods silently and slowly assembled at the foot of the snowy heights. *Madan* was put forward. He

* This was also a very celebrated *Rishi*.

† *Madan* is the god of Love.

advanced trembling from head to foot. But he gathered courage, took up his bow and sent up an arrow. It did its action ; the Great Unknown was moved ; he slowly opened his eyes and looked around. He saw the god of love, slinking away from his sight. Uncontrolable anger rose up in his bosom, and his forehead emitted forth destructive fire. Soon the poor god of love was overwhelmed with its deadly flames. Oh, how piteously he cried for help ! how he appealed to the gods to save him from *Shiva's* anger ! But the *Yoga*-sleep of the great God was destroyed. He rose from his seat and moved towards his home. At this opportune moment, when the wound made by Love was fresh in his heart, *Nârada* greeted him and proposed the marriage. He told the great God how badly the universe was faring by his inactivity and his *Yoga* ; how it had become urgently necessary for him to marry and settle down ; how his wife had again taken birth as a daughter of king *Himálaya*.

Shiva gave his consent and *Nárada* hastened to the gods to impart to them the welcome news. There was great joy amongst the gods and the goddesses ; they all hastened from all quarters to be present at the wedding. It was solemnized in due form, the Creator himself acting as the high priest.

A son was born of this marriage and he was named *Kártikeya*. When he grew up, he was elected as the general of the heavenly hosts. Under him the gods received back their old courage and energy; and under his flag they rallied round, and hoped to regain their lost heaven.

Kártikeya led the gods to the gates of heaven and challenged the demons to battle. Another great war broke out and lasted for years, till at last the great *Táraká* was killed and the demons were hopelessly defeated. They were driven out of the celestial kingdom and heaven was regained.*

[4]

TIME went on and there was no disturbance in heaven. But the struggle of elements could never cease; the deadly feud between the gods and the demons could never end in peace and amity. A decade passed when two very powerful demon were born, who gathered round them all the demon chiefs and began to disturb the peace of heaven. King *Sambhu* and his brother *Nisambhu* gradually grew very powerful and extended their sway far and wide over

* Again there is a great similarity of this tale with the tale of the Bible. *Shoma's* enticement of the heavenly goddess and the consequent loss of heaven looks almost like Satan's enticement of Eve and the loss of Paradise. Again here in this tale the heaven was regained by the birth of a son of God *Shiva*, just as in the Bible, by the birth of Christ.

the universe. They attacked more than once the gods, defeated and routed them in battle and made their position most uncomfortable and untenable in heaven. They were far more powerful than *Bitra* or *Táraká*; in fact the great Destroyer honoured them by bestowing upon them his great Spirit, which necessarily made them, on the one hand thoroughly invincible and irresistible; and on the other the very incarnation of destruction and evil. They possessed a General as great as themselves; the *Dánava Raktabija*, having secured from *Shiva* the boon of having a *Raktabija* at each drop of his blood. Thus he was more than an immortal; the gods are not killed, but the General of king *Shambhu*, if wounded, would produce a host of *Raktabijas*, as powerful as the original one.* The gods lost heart and gradually began to fly from heaven. *Indra* hastened to *Brahmá*, but he said that he really did not know what to advise. He hastened to *Vishnu* and asked permission to resign his throne and sceptre of heaven, if He did not protect him and the gods from the oppressions of *Shambhu* and *Nishambhu*. "*Indra*," said the Preserver, "Twice have I pointed to you the way to defeat the *Dánavas*.

* The Hindu *Rishis* wanted to show that the negative forces and elements grew more and more powerful as they are beaten down by the positive forces and elements. *Shambhu* and *Nishambhu* were greater heroes than *Bitra* and *Táraká*.

But really I do not know what to say now. As far as I see, *Sambhu* and *Nisambhu* cannot be killed, unless the great Destroyer does it himself. None can help you at this crisis except the Lord or the Lady of *Kailásh*."*

Who could dare go to the God of Destruction? *Indra* appeared suppliant before *Durgá*, the Lady of *Kailásh*. She was moved by the piteous appeals of the gods and the goddesses. Finding no other way to check the oppressing and destroying power of the demon kings she agreed to go and fight with them. "My dear children," said she, "Go back to your heaven; remain at ease; for the good of the world I shall go and kill these two demon kings."

She appeared as a most beautiful damsel in the pleasure-garden of the demon king. Her exceptional beauty was more than what could be described; her voluptuous grace and her youthful loveliness filled the place with a sort of majesty and grandeur.

The report of her arrival soon reached the demon-king. Great *Shambhu* grew mad to possess her; he immediately sent messengers to her, offering the throne and kingdom. But she was not what they took her to be.

* The tale shows that the negative forces were always very powerful and often they grew supreme over all others; God had to interfere to check them to keep up the equillibrium in Nature.

"Oh, beautiful lady," said the messenger, "Who art thou that hast graced our royal gardens?" The great goddess smiled and replied, "I am his who admires and adores me." "Then, Oh Lady," said the messenger, "Come to our king. I have been sent by him. He asks you to be his queen." "Go and tell him," said she, "I am only to be had by force. Whoever defeats me in battle, possesses me in peace."*

When her bold words were reported to the king he smiled and took it for a joke. But in order to humour her, he ordered one of his great generals to go to her and escort her to the royal palace. But she challenged him to battle; the poor general was forced to fight and was killed.

King *Shambhu* was really astonished to learn that his general had been killed by a woman. He was not to be trifled with; he immediately ordered another of his generals to go with his army and bring the damsel to the royal court. But there was a great battle, and the general perished with all his army.

The king was really alarmed; he sent for his Commander-in-Chief, *Raktabija* and asked him to see what the matter was. The great *Dánava* went out with all his soldiers and found the Goddess quietly sitting, after destroying the demon army. He tried to

* We would ask our readers to mark the words that fell from the lips of the Goddess. What could be truer and grander?

induce her to come with him without further ado; but she declined and challenged him to battle. "Shame on me," said *Raktabija*, "If I fight with a woman." "But" replied she, "Try the game. I am more than a woman."

At last *Raktabija* was forced to fight and a terrible battle raged from morning to night. The Great Goddess fought as the great Spirit of Destruction could possibly fight. But, alas, all her efforts were fruitless, for she could not kill *Raktabija* ;—in her efforts to kill him, she created innumerable *Raktabijas* to fight with her.

She at last appeared in her great *Kâli*-form,* she divided herself into innumerable *Kâlis*; and all those *Kális* began to fight in the greatest fury, some killing the demons and some drinking up their blood. Thus no more blood was dropped and no more *Raktabija* was created. By the evening the whole demon army with their great General had perished; and the Goddess having withdrawn her forces,had herself turned again into a beautiful damsel.

We need not say, the demon king was much alarmed and much grieved by the sad fate of his great General. He gathered round him the rest of his great army and sallied forth to fight with the fell woman, who

---

* *Káli* is the form of the Great Spirit of Destruction.

had suddenly appeared in his kingdom. We need not try to describe this battle,—a battle the equal of which had never occurred and which the greatest poet had failed to adequately describe. Suffice it to say that when the great *Shambhu* saw his beloved brother fall, he became ten times more furious and caught hold of the flowing black hair of the Great Goddess in the heat of the action; he raised her up and whirled her round by the head. She was defeated, she was mercilessly whirled and she hardly had time to breathe or to cry for help. Then she silently prayed for protection and help of his great husband *Shiva*, who soon came to her rescue. He immediately withdrew from the demon king the Spirit with which he blessed him. The great demon suddenly found him as weak as a child and was soon killed.

There was great joy amongst the gods and they lived happily in heaven.*

* There are many more wars and battles, but the three narrated above are sufficient to give an idea of the whole thing.

SHIVA AND SATI.

[1]

NORTH of the *Himálayas*, in the land of beauty and sublimity, there was a charming hill, called the *Kailásh*. It was the land of *Apsaris* and *Kinnaris*;* it was the land of many colored flowers and folliage ;—it was a lovely bower of Nature's own making, where she had congregated all that was beautiful and all that was lovely and charming in the animal or in the botanic kingdom.

In this land of love, beauty and pleasure *Shiva* and his beloved wife *Sati* had their happy home.†

---

* *Apsaris* and *Kinnaris* are beautiful races of songstresses and dancing girls.

† There is apparently some difference between *Shiva* the Destroyer as described in the preceding tale and the one that will be described in the following. Readers should know that the

It was but a cottage on the top of a snowy range; it was a hut, a poor hut covered with twining creepers. There was not to be seen the least artificial effort to secure any of the worldly comforts; but Nature was an obedient maid, in this poor but the most happy home. She gathered round the hut for their frugal meals all the sweet fruits of the world; she came with all her flowers to decorate their nuptial bed,—she placed in their lovely bower all the singing birds of the sky to pour into their ears the sweetest music of the world.

But *Shiva* had intentionally given up all that was worldly. Well, he was the richest man of the world;—he was the wisest of all the wise and the mightiest of all the mighty; he had no wants to complain of. But he had left all this far behind him and had made

---

Hindu *Rishis* have left behind them two very grand ideals of human life. They have painted two great figures, which they intended to place before the world as the best models which man can imitate and adopt, inorder to be *fully* happy in this life and to get eternal salvation in the life next. *Shiva* and *Sati* and their *Kailásh*-home is one of these two. Here *Shiva* is not the terrible Destroyer, but a great *Yogee*, a man with the highest perfection of asceticism and intellect in him. By the highest developement of asceticism he is fully happy and beyond all misery in this world; and by the highest developement of his mind he has become *one* with the Supreme Being in the next. In the next tale, readers will find quite a different sort of an ideal in the life of *Srikrishna*;—there a man is happy and saved by perfect worldliness and love.

his abode in the solitude of *Kailásh*, away from all worldly wealth and cares.

He wore a piece of tiger's skin ;—he sat on that of a lovely deer ; round his neck hung the garlands of bones ;—he was entwined with deadly snakes and serpents. He rode an old bull and begged from door to door.* He took strong narcotics and looked like a maniac. To him all the horrors of the world were welcome.

But he was a mighty man ;—he ruled over the Matter and controlled the Spirit. He was the perfect developement of Intellect ;—always deeply engaged in his own thoughts, he cared nought for the world around. He forgot that there existed a universe ;—he was intoxicated with the wine of his own thoughts ;—and that thought consisted of meditating upon his own dear wife *Sati*. He forgot that he or any other being did exist,—he felt that only ONE existed and that ONE was his lovely wife SATI.†

---

* This is but an imperfect description of the form of *Shiva*. In fact the Hindu *Rishis* tried to paint great Nature and the greater Source of that Nature in the forms of *Shiva* and *Sati*.

† This is but a faint description of one of the grandest philosophical truths of the Hindus. This is what the *Yoga* philosophy aims at. The *Vedánta* philosophy says the same. We should ask our readers, who might be curious to learn more of it, to read *Yoga* and *Vedánta* philosophies.

He had two faithful attendants, named *Nandi* and *Bhringi* ;—he was sorrounded with innumerble ghosts and spirits ; he was feared and respected all over the world. But look to the side of this horrible and fearful figure ; there you will find seated smiling and happily a goddess, quite the reverse of this terrible one.

It was *Sati*, the daughter of king *Daksha*, one of the mightiest rulers of the earth. There is no language which can adequately describe her most wonderful beauty. But no jewellery adorned her hair ; no ornaments her body. Her black long hair flowed down her back and breast in beautiful ringlets ;—round her neck there were some garlands of beads and round her loins and body was a piece of rag.

She had given up all her paternal royal luxuries, —she had become a poor beggar and a great ascetic like her husband dear. She lived with him happy and her home in *Kailásh* was the happiest in the world.

They had risen above the broils of the world ;—they had gone beyond the all-grasping hand of Mysery. They soared high in a place where nothing worldly, material or gross could reach them. They were necessarily the happiest and their home was pervaded through with perfect bliss.

They had no wants, for they had destroyed all wants ; they lived in the world, but had destroyed the idea of its existence in their minds. They achieved that grand knowledge which told them that this perceptible universe was only a mental dream of the Supreme Being, having had no real existence of its own. They felt the grand truth which told them that they were not separate beings; but they were that GREAT ONE who only is real and who only does exist.

Necessarily all worldly matters fled from their lovely home; necessarily nothing savouring of the material world could dare approach their grand *Kailásh*. They lived very happy in the Land of intellect and in the happy valley of salvation and bliss.

Thus lived *Shiva* and *Sati* for many years on the snowy heights of their happy *Kailásh*, till an unhappy incident occurred. Once on a time *Shiva* happened to attend a great *Yagma** where his father-in-law, king *Daksha*, was present. He was a man having his mind somewhere engaged. He did not observe the approach of his father-in-law and forgot to show him the proper respect. The proud

* *Yagma* was a great religious ceremony; in which a great fire which was called *Homa* was kindled and *Vedic* hymns were chanted to propitiate and to praise some particular god or all the gods. There were various sorts of *Yagmas*, in the course of which animals were sacrificed. Those *Yagmas* were very expensive affairs and only great kings could solemnise them. Amongst the modern Hindus *Yagmas* have almost died out.

king took offence ; he was never pleased with his mad son-in-law. Learning that the horrible man, whom he took to be a great *Yogee* and to whom he gave his most beloved daughter in marriage, had made his *Sati* worse than a beggar, he gave up all communication with him. He was not with him even on speaking terms ; he studiously used to avoid him and told people that his daughter was dead. But when he saw his mad son-in-law openly insulting him by not according to him the ordinary courtesy of the society, he resolved to teach him a lesson.

He held a *Yagma*, in which he invited all the world except *Shiva*, and necessarily his wife poor *Sati*. There were great preparations and grand amusements ; it was one of the greatest festivities ever held in this world ; it was a festivity in which all the people of the world were specially invited to join, except the mad man of the *Kailâsh*. All the relatives and friends of the great king came ; all the princesses of the royal household arrived from their husbands' homes, except poor *Sati*, who was not even informed of the great festivity that her beloved father was holding.

But *Nârada* went to *Kailâsh* and informed her what was going on at her father's palace. *Sati* grew eager to go,—she had not seen her mother and sisters for many years past ; she felt that her absence in this great festivity would be deeply felt by her dear mother, —if not by any one else.

She went to her husband and told him all that she had heard from *Nárada*. She entreated him to allow her to go and see her parents. "My poor darling," said *Shiva*, "Your father has purposely forgotten to invite us. He wants to heap insults over *Shiva*, to whom insults are honours. But *Sati*, why should you go and be insulted before all your relatives and friends ?" "My dear husband," replied she "Should a daughter very much mind, whether her father invites her or not ? Is there any necessity for a daughter to seek for an invitation when she goes to see her parents ?"

Shiva smiled and said, "I shall not prevent you from going to your parents. But *Sati*, remember that you are going to a great trial. Be very careful and try to come back as soon as possible." Then he turned to *Nandi* and ordered him to go with her. "*Nandi*," said he, "Take care to control your temper. There you will find all that wealth and worldly vanity can produce. You and your *Sati* will appear in that grandeur and pomp like two of the poorest beggars of the world. People may naturally redicule you,—nay they may slight you or perhaps insult you. Do not mind all this ; come back with *Sati* as soon as possible." They left *Kailásh*,—*Sati* on the back of the old Bull, *Nandi* leading him to the palace of king *Daksha*.

Beyond and above the world this asceticism is very grand; but in a place where the wealth and riches of the world had come to vie with one another, where the great chiefs and potentates had come together with all their showy costumes and invaluable jewellery, *Sati's* appearance looked like something very hateful. Especially to king *Daksha*, it was really painful,—nay insulting to find his own daughter present in that grand assembly in a plight worse than that of a beggar.

They entered the great palace, now alive with men and women. They passed through the crowd in silence, alas, none welcoming them! Their slight and neglect were apparent on all sides;—many whispered amongst themselves and many began to abuse *Shiva*, who had made a royal princess a beggar.

She went to her mother,—who came running to welcome her, she being the most beloved of all her children. But she was horrified to see the beggarly state of her daughter;—she stood a few seconds wildly staring at her and then she fainted. Then arose wild weepings all over the palace; *Sati* had come unasked and uninvited, but she had come as a beggar.

[3]

QUEEN *Prasuti* asked her daughter to give up her beggarly costume. She brought for her beautiful jewel-lery and gold-embroidered clothes,—she brought for her various delicacies, those that were her favourites when she was a child. But *Sati* declined all. "Dear mother," said she, "I must first see my father and ask him why he has not invited us ?"

She heard no refusal ; she went to the grand assembly where king *Daksha* was engaged in the great *Yagma*.

Oh, What a contrast ? Asceticism and worldliness stood side by side. The worldly pomp and grandeur stood face to face with solitude and calmness of Retirement. Poverty was placed by the side of Wealth.

Sati appeared in that grand assembly and all rose in respect. But king *Daksha* lost his temper. "Oh, shame, shame to me !" Cried he, "Why did I not die before seeing my own daughter reduced to such an ignoble state ! Who asked you to come here,—Oh you wicked girl, to me you are dead." Then he turned towards the assembly and roared. "Look at the doings of that ruffian who calls himself a *Yogee*. Mad wicked scoundrel,—always beastly drunk and piteously dirty, look, gentlemen, how he has reduced a Princess of the royal house of great *Daksha* to the lowest stratum of poverty !" "Father, dear father," appealed *Sati*, "Abuse me if you like ; but do not abuse my husband. You yourself taught me in my early days that to a wife her husband, however bad he might be, is her God and Preceptor."

But king *Daksha* fired on ; he did not care for the feelings of his poor daughter. She again and again tried to stop him,—but finally seeing that it was impossible to stop her enraged father from showering abuses over his dear husband's head,—she determined to give up her life. Death she preferred to hearing such abuses of one who was her husband.

She stood in that great assembly as only a goddess could stand ; she mentally meditated upon her husband ; she bade him farewell ; she then turned towards the assembly and fell dead.

There were loud lamentations all over the palace ; —people ran to see *Sàti* from all directions, queen *Prasuti* came weeping with all her daughters. The joy and merriments were soon turned into sorrow and grief.

In the meanwhile *Nandi* hastened to *Kailásh*. *Shiva* heard in silence of the death of his most beloved wife. He rose and madly rushed towards the kingdom of king *Daksha* followed by all his Ghosts and Spirits.

Soon the mad hordes appeared before the assembly ; in a minute the *Yagma* was destroyed, and the assembled guests were mercilessly beaten. King *Daksha* was attacked ;—he was soon beheaded and the head of a goat was placed upon his shoulder.*

* It is said that when king *Daksha* was killed, queen *Prasuti* fell at the feet of her son-in-law and wept piteously. *Shiva* was

Shiva took up the corpse of his dear wife, placed it on his shoulder and began to dance like a maniac.

He left the palace of king *Daksha* with the dead body and roamed over the world for many long years till it gradually fell piece by piece from his shoulder.*

He then silently retired to his mountain home ;—and there sat he in his great *Yoga*. He entered into that grand sleep of eternal peace which lasted for hundreds of years.†

We have already told in another tale how *Sati* was born as *Umá*, the daughter of king *Himálaya* and how she was again married to her mad husband.‡

They lived happily for years and in the strictest asceticism ; but that asceticism was mixed with the best possible domestic love and happiness.

---

moved ; he ordered *Nandi* to put life into king *Daksha's* body. But *Nandi* did not give him his original head, which was severed from his body,—for he did not like to see the face again which uttered abuses of great *Shiva*. This is the origin of the king's head becoming that of a goat.

* It was said that *Vishnu* cut off the body from his shoulder.

† Read the preceding tale.

‡ Read the tale, named the Battle of Gods and Demons.

SRIKRISHNA.

[1]

MUTTRA is one of the most important cities in the North Western Provinces. It was the capital of the kingdom of the celebrated *Yadu* Dynasty at the time when the *Kurus* and the *Pándus* were reigning in *Hastinápur*.* It is situated on the bank of the beautiful river *Yamuná* which rolls down by its side, giving beauty and health, plenty and prosperity all through the kingdom. A few miles up the river there was a splendid *Tamála* forest, where beautiful deer roamed in green pastures and rainbow-

* See the Battle of Kurukshetra.

coloured peacocks danced under the shade of flowery trees. It was the pleasant haunt of the people of Muttra ; it was the place for holding picnics for the young and the *Pujáhs* and *Yagmas* for the old. It was the place where the beautiful *Yadu* maids came to dance and play ; it was the place where the *Muttra* matrons came to while away their spare moments. In fact, this beautiful *Brindábana*, situated as it was on the bank of the rippling *Yamuná*, gardened by *Tamála, Bakul* and *Kadamba* trees, and interpersed with green pastures and shady streamlets, was the pleasure ground of the rich and the poor of the great city of *Muttra*.

On the opposite side of the river a few miles down the city there stood a very prosperous village, called *Gakula*. It was inhabited by milkmen,—a class of people always famous for their physical strength and worldly wealth. They possessed innumerable cows, bullocks and buffaloes, and lands covering many miles on the bank of the *Yamuná* were in their possession and were used as pasture-grounds for their cattle. The *Gakula* milkmen were simple, virtuous and honest ; none of them was poor, but none was very rich. They had their own society, in which they lived independent and happy. Their women were beautiful and lovely, honest and simple, but bold and forward in demeanour. Health, plenty and beauty reigned in *Gakula* ; surely it was a place where gods might fancy to come and live.

At the time of which we are speaking, *Nanda* was the head of this Dairy clan. None was so good and none was so fit to be the patriarch of this wild but simple people as he ; and he was truly matched in all his good qualities by his wife *Yasodá*. They were loved and respected, nay feared and obeyed, by all the people of *Gakula*. And his influence was so great that he commanded respect even from the members of the royal family, who ruled in *Muttra*. King *Kansa* was then the reigning sovereign, a ruler hated of his subjects and feared by his enemies. He was a base and heartless tyrant ; he was a monster of iniquity and demon of cruelty. The people groaned under his tyranny and oppression ; but he was very powerful, and none there was in the kingdom who dared breathe a word against him.

[2]

AS in the case of every tyrant, king *Kansa* was always afraid and suspicious of all the people amongst whom he had to live and move. He always feared, lest he might be killed by his enemies ; he took special care to know from every possible quarter whether he had any fear from any man and if so, whom to fear ; so that he might take previous precaution to ward them off. He was told by astrologers that his sister *Debaki's* eighth son would kill him ; and he had none else to fear.* As soon as he learnt it, he imprisoned his sister and her husband, *Basudeva*, intending to kill them,so that no son might be born to them. But they fell at his feet and craved for mercy ; they promised on solemn oath that they would deliver to him all the children born to them, and they would not complain, if he would kill them as soon as they were born. The cruel king was moved and he agreed to the stipulation,† but kept them prisoners in his own palace, well guarded, so that they might not secretly remove their children.

One after another seven children were born and duly delivered to the cruel tyrant, who to make his safety doubly sure killed them all. But the poor parents determined to save the eighth ; whatever be the consequence they determined to make an effort

* There are some other versions of this foretelling ;—but from whatever source it might be, king *Kansa* came to know his fate many years before it did occur.

† The eighth son of *Basudeva* and *Debaki* is *Srikrishna*, a personage worshipped and adored by the Hindus as an incarnation of God. We need not say that there are various versions of his birth and life. We need not also tell our readers that there are more than one miracle mentioned all through the narrative of his life. We shall avoid mentioning for obvious reasons the miracles in the body of this tale, but would mention them in short notes.

to save at least one of their beloved children from the wrath of their cruel relative and king. When at the dead of night their eighth child, which was a very beautiful boy, was born, *Vasudeva* wrapped it up in clothes, took it under his arms and stealthily came out of the prison-house.* It was an awful night;—the blue sky was full of black clouds; the lightning was flashing and the thunder was roaring; the rain was falling like torrents, and the wind was blowing in mad fury. It was the eighth day of the full moon in the month of *Bhádra*,† the very middle of the rainy season. The *Yamuná* had risen, and she had almost flooded her banks. In this fearful night when Nature was dancing in her wild fury, *Vasudeva* with his child under his arms hastened towards the village of *Gakula*, and came to the bank of the rushing, roaring and foaming river.‡ Somehow he managed

* It is said that both *Vasudeva* and *Debaki* heard the voice of God who asked them to save the child and told them how to do it. It is further said that He made the guards fall into a deep sleep and opened the door Himself. There are some more miracles narrated in connection with this birth, which we need not mention.

† Corresponding to August.

‡ It is said that when *Vasudeva* was meditating how to cross the river he saw a jackal walking across it. He followed the animal's example and found to his joy that the water of the river was very shallow. It was also said that a big snake walked all the way with him protecting the child from rain by its big fangs.

to cross it; he ran towards the house of *Nanda,* whose wife *Yashodá* had given birth to a daughter that very night. None was astir,—none could possibly be astir in that dreadful night; *Yashodá* was in deep sleep in her lying-in room, her new-born child lying by her side. *Vasudeva* stealthily entered into that room and placed his own boy by her side; he took up the daughter of the milkman and hastened back home.* None knew what was done at the dead of night. The child that would kill the cruel king was thus saved. *Kansa* found in the morning that a daughter was born to his sister. He brought it out and ordered it to be killed.†

[3.]

THE son of *Vasudeva* and *Devaki* was tenderly nursed by *Yashodá* and carefully brought up by *Nanda.* The prince of the royal house of *Yadu* grew up as one of the milkman's boys of *Gakula.*‡ He

---

* It is mentioned that God made *Yashodá* and all the people of *Gakula* fall into a deep sleep. We need not say that it is also told that *Vasudeva* was previously directed by the voice of God to make this exchange of children.

† It is said that when the people dashed the child on a piece of stone to kill it, it flew from their hands and rose up into the sky.

‡ We must here remind our readers that the character of *Krishna* is an ideal life placed before humanity. We shall refer them to our notes in the tale, named *Shiva* and *Sati.* As they have

was the joy of all the village; and the milkmen and the milkmaids gave him various names, of which we shall mention only two. He was called *Kánái* by his mother and he was known by the name of *Krishna* all through his clan.

What possible education the son of a milkman could reasonably get? Learning was not in their line; their children had no idea of entering into the deep labyrinths of Science, Philosophy, or Literature. *Krishna* was sent out to take care of the cattle in the pasture, as soon as he grew up to the age of doing it; and he daily went out with all the other boys of the village. But although he learnt nothing, he learnt at least one thing; it was to play on the flute;—the flute that maddened the maids of *Gakula* and which in after-life turning into a conch* sent inspiration into the hearts of heroes on bloody fields of battle.

Well, the beautiful *Yamuná* flowed by *Gakula* giving it health and plenty; but with the birth of *Krishna* a streamlet of Love flowed through the milkmen's village giving it untold pleasure and

---

found in that tale an ideal character of *asceticism* in perfection, they will find in this a quite opposite character, namely an ideal character of *worldliness* in perfection. There they have found *first asceticism* and then in that great *asceticism* great love; here they will find *first* great love and then in that great love great *worldliness*.

* Conch served the purpose of a bugle in ancient warfare.

eternal bliss. The baby *Krishna* was the darling of his mother and the joy of all the villagers. The child *Krishna* was the caressing idol of all the women and the boy *Krishna* was the most beloved companion and play-mate of all the boys. The men and women of *Gakula* knew not why they began to love *Krishna* in a way the reason of which they could not account for. They loved their own children, but their love towards *Krishna* was something more than usual,—nay it was more than what could be found in Nature. And how naughty he was ! He was not a good boy ; neither he was gentle, nor mild. He would enter into his neighbours' houses, make havock on the eatables,—specially on milk and butter,—break household utensils and do a thousand other mischiefs. So great was their love towards him that they suffered in silence, never complaining for his misdeeds or any of his wicked pranks.* But his pranks amongst his neighbours soon ceased. Though

* We must here narrate at least two of the miracles that took place in his childhood. Once a sorceress, named *Putanâ*, was sent by *Kansa* to kill him by allowing him to suck her poisonous breasts, but the child killed her. On another occasion *Yashodâ* wanted to tie his hands with a rope, so that he might not do any mischief in the neighbours' houses ; but all the ropes of the house were brought, (and a milkman's supply of rope must be considerable) but was found not enough to bind up his two hands.

Yashodá was not at all willing,—yet *Krishna* was forced to go out into the field to look after his father's cattle. How unwillingly and with how much reluctance she sent him out ! How many times she imploringly asked him not to go very far, not to go near the dangerous water of the *Yamuná*, not to go across the river,—for she was afraid of king *Kansa*,—not to roam under the hot sun and not to do a thousand other things ! She gave him eatables, those that she knew her darling *Krishna* was fond of ; how many times she tenderly requested him to eat them when he would feel hungry ! She would stand at the gate and look at him,—as only a loving mother looks at her departing boy,—as he sped along with his play-mates, driving the cattle before him.

The boys grew mad for him ; they would not go to the pasture without their beloved *Kánái* ; no play could be played without him, no game was managed without his presence. He was their leader, he was their friend,—nay he was their all. He led them to many plays, he invented many games ; he enchanted them with his love, he amused them with his sweet flute.*

* There are many anecdotes told regarding this period of his life. Some of them are possible facts, but many of them are miracles. He showed at this early period of his life superhuman physical strength and sometimes mysterious powers. He killed

[4]

THUS *Krishna* slowly and gradually spread around him a halo of love and created a new world of bliss. Thus when he entered into his teens, he drew all the maids of *Gakula* towards him. His beauty, his grace, his amiability and love, over and above all this, his sweet and enchanting music on his magic flute, made them unconsciously love him.

They met him on their way to the river,—in the morning when they went to bathe and in the evening when they went to fetch water in their pitchers. They began to converse with him, they began to loiter with him,—nay they sometimes passed some hours with him in merry-making. One after another they all fell in love with him, and *Krishna* loved them all. *Krishna* and the lovely maids of *Gakula* were slowly carried away into the blissful whirlpool of love.*

many demons, specially the demonaic snake *Kália* who used to live under the water in a certain place in the *Yamuná*. Many of the cattle of *Gakula* died by drinking the poisonous water of this place. *Krishna* one day jumped into this poisonous pool, dived down and killed the fearful snake-demon.

* This love affair has been variously described, sometimes with questionable taste and purity ; but readers should know that *Srimat Bhágabata*, one of the best Sanskrit Works, is the chief authority on the life of *Srikrishna*. We find nothing objectionable,—in fact there was not the least trace of carnality—in this grand love as described in this book,—a love in which not one but all the

In the day *Krishna* was surrounded by his play-mates, and the maids had also their household duties to perform. They could only see him on their way to the *Yamuná* and pass a few minutes with him, which did not satisfy their cravings for his sweet company. They began to meet him at night, and specially at moon-lit night, in the surrounding gardens and orchards,—and sometimes on the green pasture. There they played and amused themselves with their lover in various ways. His flute was the signal for a general rush towards the beautiful groves, where there was nothing but love and pleasure. *Krishna* organised plays, games and picnics in the gardens and groves for the amusements of the maids, as he did for the boys on the pasture grounds. Of these various games and merry-makings, only two we shall mention. In the rainy season he organised a grand swing-play, and in the spring a great red powder contest, in both of which all the boys and maids of *Gakula* heartily joined.*

women living on both the banks of the *Yamuná* percipitated. In fact *Srikrishna* was almost a boy at the time when this love affair is said to have taken place.

* Both of these two occasions are observed by the Hindus as great religious festivals; one is called *Jhulana* and the other *Hori* or *Dola*.

His plays and games, his sweet music, his universal love, drew round him hundreds of maids, not only of *Gakula*, not only of his own clan, but from far and wide. From the villages on both the banks of the river, nay from the *Muttra* city itself, boys and girls came flocking to him,—to love him,to adore him, to enjoy the heavenly bliss which he was freely distributing to all.

Then he organised a grand moon-light ball,* not in the orchards and gardens of *Gakula*, but in the magnificent parks of *Brindábana* itself,the place of recreation and amusements,—the pleasure gardens,— of the great city. The day fixed was the full moon of autumn,† when the moon shines in all her glory;—the time the moon-lit night,—the place the *Brindábana*, watered by the silvery *Yamuná*, and beautified by flowery plants and many-coloured folliage. In this ever charming place the grand *Rásha*‡ was held; all the lovely maidens of the neighbourhood, in their best attire and bedecked with all the flowers and

* This occasion is also observed as a great religious festival every year. *Brindábana* is held to be a celebrated place of pilgrimage on account of *Krishna's* holding his celebrated dance at this place.

† It is the full moon day of *Agraháun* and generally falls in the month of October.

‡ *Rásha* leterally means a dance.

perfumes, came and joined in this grand dance. Great Poets have failed adequately to describe this magnificent affair,—it is better for us not to attempt a thing, left undone by greater personages.*

[5]

KRISHNA'S kingdom of love did not consist of only boys and girls, child and woman. All the milkmen of his own clan,—nay the people of all castes and creeds,—sacrificed themselves at the altar of his great love. In fact they made an unconditional surrender to him in all matters;—love rose above the ties of relation, above the rules of social etiquette, and above every other worldly consideration. The old and the young, nay even the venerable Patriarchs, bowed at his feet; they honoured and respected him as thier leader and chief. It would suffice if we

* We must mention here that in many *Purânas*, except *Bhágabata*, it is mentioned that out of all the maidens one named *Rádhá* loved him most and *Krishna* too loved her the best. But in *Bhágabata* no mention of *Rádhá* is made; in fact there we find *Krishna's* love spreading to all equally and impartially, he having not the least preference for any special girl or woman. It is said that *Rádhá* was his maternal aunt and the wife of one *Āyâna*. There are many anecdotes in connection with *Rádhá's* love for *Krishna*. At the present time *Krishna* is worshipped along with *Rádhá*, and she is to be found by his side in every temple.

mention only one event; it will prove the extent of his influence over the people amongst whom he lived.

He preached thoroughly a new religion,—a religion thoroughly novel and thoroughly subversive of all their cherished beliefs and faiths. He preached against the time-honoured ancient religion and advocated Nature-worship. But so great was their love for him,that they submitted to him,though a mere boy, even for the future welfare of their souls;—they trampled down their old religion and followed him to do things, novel and new. They accompanied him to the hill *Gobardhana,* there to worship Nature.*

We need not say that such doings do not remain hidden. The name of *Krishna* passed from house to house; his great deeds became the general topics of conversation; his fame spread all over the kingdom of *Muttra.* King *Kansa* was alarmed; though he attempted to kill *Krishna* more than once, and sent emissaries for the purpose yet he did not take him to be a very dangerous personage. But now he grew

---

* It is said that when *Krishna* with his clan and his followers both male and female went to worship *Gòbardhana*, God *Indra* took offence; for the *Gakula* people openly gave up the worship of gods and godesses. He ordered raining, and it rained in torrents for seven nights and seven days. *Krishna* saved his people from this deluge by raising up the hill which he kept on his little finger. All the people rested under it and were thus saved. Hill *Gobardhana* stands about 30 miles from *Muttra.*

really alarmed; and his alarm was hundred-fold increased when he heard that *Krishna* was not the son of *Nanda,* but that of *Vasudeva,*—the very boy to kill whom he had killed innumerable children. His anger knew no bounds; but he controlled himself, for he knew that *Krishna* had become an idol of worship to all the people of Muttra. An open attempt to kill him now meant a general revolt of all his subjects. He also feared that his soldiers would not fight with *Krishna,* but would go over to his side. So he determined to kill him treacherously. Any how this great enemy he thought of removing.

There was a man named *Akrur* in *Muttra* who loved *Krishna* and whom *Krishna* loved. King *Kansa* called him to his court; he received him with all honour and bestowed upon him many presents. "Good and virtuous *Akrur,*" said he, "I have been informed that *Krishna* is the son of my sister. I should no longer allow him to remain as a milkman's boy. He should at once come and live in *Muttra,* as a prince of my great house should live. I am told that *Krishna* loves you much; and therefore I have resolved to send you to him to bring him with all honour to my royal court, so that he might henceforth assume his own exalted position."

Akrur went to *Gakula* with the royal message; there was joy and lamentation all over the beautiful village,—joy for *Krishna's* elevation and lamentation for his departure. But he consoled them all, gave them hopes that he would soon return and went to *Muttra* in *Akrur's* chariot.*

The king received him most graciously; he welcomed him in all pomp and grandeur; he made arrangements for various amusements for his reception. One of these was a pugilistic fight, in which *Krishna* was asked to join. The king privately gave instruction to kill him on the spot, but *Krishna* soon learnt his nefarious intention,—the assembled people also understood the king's evil intention and rose in a body.

Krishna easily killed the murderous pugilists and then he attacked the wicked king and killed him on the spot. There were great uproars and confusions; and amidst the general acclamation he was placed on the throne of *Muttra* with the unanimous consent of the people.

[6]

We now come to the second period of his life.† He has forgotten all his early boyish pranks and has turned a grave statesman; he has become a powerful

---

* This occasion is also observed as a religious festival.

† The first period of *Krishna's* life is full of love, the second full of worldliness.

and able ruler. He has forgotten his loving play-mates, his lovely maidens, his obedient adorers, nay even his mother *Yashodá* and father *Nanda*. When they all came to his royal palace to take him back to his old haunts, he told them as prince *Harry* told his boon companions.

> "Presume not that I am the thing I was,
> —I have turned away my former-self."

The days of love-making were gone; the days of playing, merry-making and amusing were over; *Krishna* had much to do in the field of politics. The whole of India had been torn by internal dissensions; tyrants had become all powerful and merciful rulers had disappeared. The people had fled into the deepest forest to save themselvs from the oppressions of wicked men. When *Krishna* found himself on the throne of *Muttra* he saw all this in a glance; he thought he could do much to protect the oppressed and bestow peace and happiness all over India. He had become a ruler of a province,—why, he could be the ruler of all India too! He could bring under his standard all the contending factions; he could chastise the tyrants and help the good. Indeed he found he had enough works to do, if he wanted to extend and spread a kingdom of love and happiness all over the country. The vast continent of India was not a *Gakula*; to do in this vast empire what he did in his own country village, required unknowable state-craft, and unsurpassing intelligence ; in short he required a great head and a broad heart.

Both those things he possessed. His change of character was so sudden that all the people were taken aback. When his play-mates came to his royal court, he told them gravely that his life at *Gakula* had ended, that he was no longer their loving play-mate and leader, but their king and sovereign. He asked them to go back and try to amuse the *Gakula* maidens by doing what he used to do. When weeping the broken-hearted maidens came to his door, he most seriously told them to go back ; he requested them to forget him and try to be happy without him. When his bereaved mother *Yashodá* with *Nanda* and his clan appeared at his court, he asked them to consider him no longer their son, but as a prince of the great *Yadu* dynasty and as their present king, sovereign and chief.

There were lamentations all over *Gakula*,—but there was joy all over the kingdom of *Muttra*. Both the lamentation and the joy arose out of the great love that the people bore for him. The people of *Gakula* could not bear his absence ; would they be able to live without seeing him often ! The people of *Muttra* rejoiced, because their beloved *Krishna* had at last become their ruler and king. The cruel and hard-hearted tyrant *Kansa* was killed and the great and the good *Krishna* had become their sovereign ;—what could be there in the wide world more welcome than this !

We now find him consolidating his kingdom. In order to secure powerful allies, he had married more than one royal princess. First he married *Kubjá*, then *Rukmini*, then *Shatyabhámá* and others,—all born of royal parents. He had increased his army and raised up a great and most powerful contingent out of the strong and brave milkmen of *Gakula*. He had made his subjects happy, without which no ruler could be invincible and secure. In order to make himself more qualified to interfere and meddle with foreign politics, in order to extend his power and influence beyond the limit of his own kingdom, without being anxious for its own safety and security, he removed his capital to *Dwáraká*, a city in *Gujrat*, situated on the shore of the blue ocean.

[7.]

A FEW years after we find his figure towering above the heads of all. We need not mention how he managed to raise himself up to this lofty height. We find him at this period a man, whose friendship was to be desired, whose favours were to be prayed for ; whose smiles were to be looked after and whose frowns were to be feared. Great potentates and powerful chiefs vied with one another to do him honour. Unquestionably he had become the first man of India. Why should we speak of other chiefs and potentates ? Even the great *Kurus* and *Pándus*, who were the most powerful, nay the *de facto* Imperial Dynasty of India, had fully submitted to his leadership. They considered themselves honoured to get his friendship and favour. *Bhíshma*, the Patriarch of this great dynasty, the acknowledged first warrior and statesman of the period, had acknowledged him to be an incarnation of God and adored and worshipped him as such.* From the hoary *Himálaya* to the island city ;† from *Dwáraká* to *Kámákshá*‡ he had become the Ruler of all rulers. He held in his hand both the keys of Indian politics and religion. His great intelligence was admired and submitted to ; his great love was adored and worshipped.

The internal dissensions, that were rending the country from one corner to the other, had been all settled up by him ; the tyrants had been chastised and forced to be merciful ; peace and prosperity had appeared where there were bloodshed and misery

* Read the Battle of *Kurukshetra.*

† It refers to *Lanká*, the ancient capital of Ceylon. Read Monkey War.

‡ This city still exists ; it is near Gowhatti in Assam.

And all this he did,—not by any physical force,—not by issuing forth with arms and ammunitions, with infantry and cavalry, with horses and elephants, but by simple statesmanship. Hardly ever he himself fought a battle; he managed all this through his great intelligence and magnificent state-craft.

The people of India had become very wicked and vicious; they had been spoiled without any hope of redemption or reformation. The virtuous and the good had retired into the jungle or had been living in misery and woe. *Krishna* resolved to exterminate these men from the face of the earth and thus to save India from future miseries and oppressions.

Amongst these, there were two, equal to whom there was none so bad or wicked. These were the kings *Jarásandha* and *Shishupála*. He himself killed the latter and the former was killed by the *Pandu* Princes. Thus one after another all wicked tyrants with their bad followers and subjects were exterminated from the face of the earth. But still the works of *Krishna* had not been finished. There were two most wicked and vicious clans still left to be exterminated. But both of them were very dear and near to him. One was the great *Kuru* Dynasty with its most powerful and extensive retinue, and the other was his own *Yadu* dynasty with his own children and grand children.

The powerful *Kurus* were exterminated in the great battle of *Kurukshetra.** If *Krishna* were not present with his great state-craft, in the battle to help the poor *Pándus*, it would have been impossible for them to gain the victory. He not only made his friend *Arjuna* victorious by helping him with his advice and making him do things which he would never have done, but he preached to him a religion in support of those most unscrupulous advices, based on very peculiar morals.† In fact *Krishna* asked the *Pándus* to trample down every sort of moral virtues; he asked them to kill parents, preceptors, brahmins brothers, cousins, males, females and children. To do this he advised them to adopt every sort of treachery and to take recourse to every sort of subterfuges and falsehood. His life, from the day he ascended the throne of Muttra, was a moral mystery. It was evident that his sole aim and only aim was to exterminate from the earth all the vicious and the wicked. It

* As we have written the history of this battle in another tale, we shall not repeat it here. We refer our readers for the particulars to that tale.

† We should ask our readers to read *Gitá*. When *Arjuna* seeing the battle field, declined to fight—as he thought he would have to kill his uncle, who was more than a father to him, his preceptor, who was a *Brahmin* and his dear and near relative and friend *Krishna* gave him some instructions and preached to him some moral doctrines. The *Gitá* contains these instructions.

was clearly apparent from every work of his life that his sole aim was to create a new world,—a world of love, happiness and bliss. But he himself appeared to be a man without a heart and without any feelings;—a man who was an incarnation of *worldliness*;—a man who, to serve his purpose, could do any and every sort of diabolical thing. He was a contradiction of moral faculties,—nay, he was a great mystery.

If he had disappeared from the world without explaining his religion and morals, he would have been taken for one of the worst men ever born. But in the field of the great battle of *Kurukshetra*, when his friend *Arjuna* absolutely declined to follow his peculiar morals, he was forced to explain and support his novel doctrines with arguments. And they were so convincing, they were so true and grand, that thenceforth he was universally adored and worshipped as the great incarnation of the Supreme Being.* His religion became the religion of the humanity.

---

* *Krishna's* philosophy and doctrines were, as we said, explained in the great book *Gitá*, now translated into almost all European languages. Scholars and philosophers have unanimously said that it was the grandest book of the world. We should earnestly ask our readers to read this book. We can give only a brief summary of it in the Appendix.

[8]

In the range of history or fiction we have never come across such a grand and great character. He was a lover, a thorough worldly man, a great politician and statesman, a philosopher and a prophet. Being a milkman's boy he rose to be the greatest man of India,—he became the Ruler of all rulers, the Prophet of all prophets and the Philosopher of all philosophers. But if he became all this for self-agrandisement, if these were the results of his supernatural ambition,—then of course he would have commanded very little respect from good and sensible men.

But, no,—self was not in him ; there was not the least selfishness in his actions. As we have said, his sole aim was to create a new world of love peace, happiness and bliss. To accomplish this he had to do many things and had to assume many characters—to create a world of happiness and bliss meant the extermination of the wicked and the vicious. If he spared his relatives,—his own ehildren and grand-children, we would have questioned his honesty of purpose. But, no,—he did spare none,—not even himself. He exterminated the *Kurus*, his very near relatives and friends ; he then exterminated his own great clan with his own dear sons and grandsons.

He took them all to the great pilgrimage of *Pravásha.* There was great joy and mirth in *Dwáraká.* The *Pravásha* was a place most holy, most beautiful and most enjoyable. Every one of the clan, every son and grand-son of *Krishna,* every prince of the royal *Yadu* house, made himself ready to go to the *Pravásha.* Many eatables were taken, innumerable casks of liquor followed ;—nothing was there wanting to make the pilgrimage most enjoyable and pleasant.

They all came and encamped in the holy place ; they performed the religious ceremonies, they distributed alms and fed the Brahmins. Then they began to percipitate in merry-making ;—they ate, they drank, they played, they danced. They got themselves so very drunk that soon they quarrelled amongst themselves. One abused another, the other retorted ; they fought and one was killed. His friends rose in a body and attacked the murderer,—his friends rushed to his rescue. There were great confusions,—there was bloodshed all around ; the *Yadu* princes fell on all sides as so many leaves of trees. *Krishna* was appealed to,—he was asked to stop the family fued and the bloody carnage. But he too joined in the fray and began to kill his own sons and grandsons. Soon the whole clan was exterminated ; there was none left alive except *Krishna.* When there was none to kill, *Krishna,* coolly took a view of the bloody field and moved away.*

Then he asked his charioteer to go to *Hastinápura* and inform his friend *Arjuna* what had happened. "Tell him," said he, "that all the *Yadus* are dead. Ask him in my name to hasten to *Dwáraká*, where the widowed *Yadu* princesses are left unprotected. Tell him to take them to *Hastinápura* and give them protection."

It was evident that he had no mind to return to his capital. Perhaps he thought his occupation was gone ; perhaps he thought his work was done. He slowly moved away and left the place where all that was dear and near to him fell.

---

* There is an anecdote in connection with this extermination of *Yadu* Dynasty. The *Yadus* grew so very wicked and vicious, that once when they saw a great *Rishi*, they determined to cut jokes at him. One of them assumed the garb of a female ; and the wicked *Yadu* boys took the disguised prince to the *Rishi*. They asked him to say what child the girl would give birth. The *Rishi* took offence for their irreligious behaviour and said, "Oh wicked boys, there will be born out of this one an iron rod, which would be the death of your vicious clan." The *Yadus* were alarmed, they went to *Krishna* and asked his advice. He told them to take the iron rod to *Pravásha*, rub it on a stone and thus gradually annihilate it. They did as they were asked to do. But out of the broken pieces of this rod grew long grasses in *Pravásha*. When the *Yadus* were fighting amongst themselves,—

He came to a tree, sat under it and fell asleep ;*—soon there appeared a hunter, who saw his reclining figure from a distance through the thick leaves of the tree. He mistook him for a game, took aim and shot.

There in the deep forest under the green leaves of the tree the greatest man of the age was mortally wounded ; there he breathed his last unknown and uncared for. The man, whose smile was sun-shine to all the good and whose frowns were the death-signal for all the wicked, not of *Dwáraká*, not of *Mathurá*, not of *Hastinápura*, but of all India from one corner to the other,—died in the same obscurity from which he rose.

Krishna suggested to them to use this grass as weapons. They became thunder in their hands and destroyed the whole clan.

* It is said that this sleep of *Krishna* was *Yoga*-sleep—a state in which a man, or rather his soul, joins and mixes with the Great *Soul*. It is impossible for a man to fall asleep just after the total annihilation of all his sons and grandsons ; but *Krishna* is said to have fallen asleep. Every part of his wonderful life is a mystery.

THE MONKEY WAR.

[1]

IN the modern province of Oudh there was in ancient time a powerful kingdom, called *Ayodhyá*. It was beautiful and fertile, watered by many rivers and rivulets ; its people were happy and rich, ruled by the benign Solar Princes.

Of all the kings of the great Solar Dynasty, Raja *Daçaratha* was the mightiest and the best. He was invincible in arms and unequalled in alms. The people of *Ayodhyá* were very happy to live under his kind sway ; but the king himself was not happy. He had three good wives, named *Kauçalyá, Kaikeyi* and *Sumitrá,* but none of them gave birth to a prince, who could ascend the throne of the great kingdom and rule the people, as only the Solar princes knew how to do. The people prayed and the king offered sacrifices to the gods, but time wore on and no prince was born.

Once on a time king *Daçaratha* went out a-hunting; he saw a stag, put spurs to his horse and pursued him. Soon his escorts were left behind and he disappeared into the deep forest. He at last found himself unattended and alone, the stag having disappeared from his view. He advanced and found a beautiful rivulet gliding fast; he thought he saw the stag; he aimed and shot.

"Oh, I am killed!" was uttered by the faltering voice of a boy; the king was surprised and bewildered; he ran to the place from which the piteous cry arose. What was his horror when he found that his deadly arrow had pierced the heart of a beautiful boy! He took up the boy on his lap; he tried to bind up the wound, from which hot blood was flowing like water; he tried a hundred means to save the boy, but all was to no effect.

The boy slowly raised up his head and said, "My parents are blind and old. They are fasting from yesterday and they are thirsty. Oh Sir, kindly take this pitcher of water to them and tell them that their beloved *Sindhu* is no more."

The king took up the corpse of the poor boy; he took the pitcher of water and went to the old *Rishi's* hut. His heart was palpitating and his steps were faltering,—but what was his agony when he heard the blind parents talking of their absent boy!

"Where is my *Sindhu*?" said the poor mother, "He never loiters anywhere." The old and blind father raised up his feeble voice and said, "*Sindhu*, my darling boy, come quick; I am very thirsty."

The king gathered strength and approached the bereaved parents. He broke the sad news and tried to explain that it was all an accident. "Oh, wicked man," cried the old *Rishi*, "Die,—die for the bereavement of your son and know what it is." They both died and went to the place where their beloved *Sindhu* had preceded them.

The king returned home, not very much worse for the sad occurrence, for he had no son to lose or mourn. A few months after, he went out to fight an enemy and was mortally wounded in the battle. He was carried to his palace and was most tenderly nursed by his second wife *Kaikeyi*. He was so pleased with her that he pressed her to ask for two favours, which he promised to grant her. "No, my lord," said she, "I have no wants now. If I want anything in future, I shall remind you of your kind promise."

None gave any importance to these two little incidents when they occured, but they produced great and memorable events many years after.

[2]

SOON after the king's recovery it was rumoured all over the kingdom that all the three queens were in the family-way. Some months passed and *Kauçalyá* gave birth to a boy who was named *Ráma*. Then *Kaikeyi* gave birth to a son who was named *Bharata*. The youngest queen gave birth to a twin and the boys were named *Lakshmana* and *Satrughna*.

As the boys grew up, *Lakshmana* was greatly attached to *Ráma*, and *Satrughna* to *Bharata*. They were brought up in all the accomplishments befitting their rank and station in life.

When *Ráma* was about sixteen years of age, great *Rishi Viçwámitra* came to *Ayodhyá* and asked the king to allow him to take *Ráma* to fight with the *Rákshasas*. Now *Rákshasas* were a wild race; *Rávana* was their great king. His seat was at *Lanká* in Ceylon, but he was a most powerful king with immense wealth and innumerable soldiers. In fact he subdued all the kings and potentates of India as far as the *Himálayas*. His power was irresistible and his oppressions were unbearable; he placed his relatives all over the country with instructions to rob the people and kill the Brahmins.

The uncle of king *Rávana* named *Kálnemi*, with his wild sister *Táraká*, was placed near the holy place where *Rishi Viçwámitra* had his seat. Their oppressions becoming unbearable, the venerable *Rishi* repaired to *Ayodhyá* and asked for protection. *Ráma* was only sixteen years of age, but he entreated his father to allow him to go with the *Rishi*, so that he might protect the Brahmins from trouble. King *Daçaratha* gave permission with reluctance and *Ráma* left *Ayodhyá* accompanied by his beloved brother *Lakshmana*.

They came to a great forest, where the most furious and terrible *Táraká* used to live. As soon as the Prince challenged the *Rákshashee* to fight, she rushed forward to kill him ; but *Ráma* soon killed the fell demoness ; and her brother fled away for his life. The *Rishis* gathered round the scions of the Solar Dynasty and blessed them for their great deeds.

Thence they repaired to a place called *Mithilá*, the kingdom of king *Janaka*. He had made a vow that whoever would be able to break the bow, left by *Parasuráma*,* would marry his beautiful daughter,

* *Parasuráma* was the great Brahmin who became a very powerful warrior. When the *Kshatryas* became very vicious, Brahmin *Parasuráma* took arms to chastise them. It is said that

named *Sitá*. Many princes came to secure the damsel, but none could raise the bow,—what of breaking it. *Rishi Viçwámitra* was proud of his young hero; he took him to the palace of the king and asked him to secure the Princess. *Ráma* broke the bow amidst the acclamations of all the people of *Mithilá*.

King *Janaka* received the princes in all honour; he sent ambassadors to *Ayodhyá* to apprize the old king of his son's glorious feat and to invite him to come to *Mithilá* to celebrate the nuptials. King *Daçaratha* came with all his generals and ministers. There were great festivities and *Ráma* married *Sitá*, his three brothers marrying the three sisters of the young Princess.

[3]

As *Ráma* grew up the king allowed him to govern the people, so that he might gradually learn the art of Government. His rule was so benign that all the people grew enamoured of him; they could give their lives for him, if he so willed. King

he exterminated the *Kshatryas* twenty-one times from the face of the earth. He was a terror to all *Kshatryas* and was supposed to be an incarnation of *Shiva*.

Daçaratha was much pleased to see the fame his son had thus acquired ; he ordered it to be declared all over the kingdom that *Ráma* would be made *Jubaráj** and the king would retire,—leaving the Government in his hand. Oh, the joy of *Ayodhyá* ! There were festivities in every town,—illuminations in every village and bonfires on every house top. There were music and songs ; there were distributions of alms and celebrations of *pujáhs*. In thousand and one ways the people expressed their joy for the happy news.

But alas ! there was a very wicked maid-servant, named hunch-back *Manthará*, attached to the house hold of queen *Kaikeyi*. She went to her mistress and plied her with evil advices. "Oh queen," said she, "If *Ráma* becomes king, what will be your and your *Bharata's* fate ? No better than that of beggars ! Who could ever love the son of a step-mother ? *Ráma* will imprison him, banish him or perhaps kill him ! If you now lose the opportunity, you shall have to weep till death." *Kaikeyi* was moved, she began to be convinced of the truth of her words ; she finally agreed to accept her evil advices. "What can I do," asked the queen, "to avert this great evil ?" "Do you not remember," replied the wicked woman, "the

---

* *Jubaráj* is the heir-apparent.

king promised to grant you two favours? Ask by one to place *Bharata* on the throne and by another to banish *Ráma* for fourteen years."

When the old king came to see his queen, he found her weeping and lying on the floor. He raised her up; he consoled her and tried to know the cause of her grief. Being repeatedly pressed by the king, she at last gave vent to her pent-up feelings. The poor old king heard in silence the cold and piercing words of the queen; his head reeled and his eyes swam. "Oh *Ráma*" he cried and fell flat on the ground.

Soon the sad news got wind; it spread from house to house till it reached the cottage of the poorest peasant. All festivities were stopped; the people silently and eagerly tried to know the final orders of the king. As soon as *Ráma* came to learn the cause of his father's grief and his step-mother's demand, he went to him and asked his permission to leave *Ayodhyá*. "Father," said the Prince, "if a son cannot fulfill his father's promise, what is his life worth for? Let *Bharata* have the throne, he deserves it as much as I. I shall pass fourteen years in asceticism at the expiration of which I shall return and bow at your feet." The poor old king could not utter a word. "My dear boy," said *Kaikeyi*, "Don't make your father false to his words. Go, leave

Ayodhyá." "My mother," replied *Ráma*, "I must go. Bless me, so that I might have strength enough to fulfill my father's promise."

He came out and told his beloved brother and companion, *Lakshmana*, all that had happened. "My dear *Lakshmana*," said the prince, "Remain in *Ayodhyá* and be a son to my poor mother." But the young prince could not suppress his feelings; tears rushed out of his eyes,—anger displayed itself on his countenance. "Brother," cried he, "Why should we allow a step-mother to do such an injustice? If brother *Bharata* take his wicked mother's part, I shall fight with him and make you sit on the throne." *Ráma* smiled and said, "*Lakshmana*, *Bharata's* mother is our mother. *Bharata* is as beloved to me as you. I must leave *Ayodhyá* to fulfill our father's promise. Remain here, be obedient to mother *Kaikeyi* and brother *Bharata*; love them as you love me." *Lakshmana* fell at his brother's feet, wept and entreated him to take him as his companion. "Dear brother," said he, "Do not leave me behind." *Ráma* was moved, he agreed to allow the young prince to accompany him.

We need not describe the meeting of *Ráma* with his poor mother. Oh, how happy had she been a minute before and how miserable now! He bade her adieu in tears amidst the loud lamentations of all the women of the palace. He then proceeded to bid farewell to his dear wife. There were no tears in her eyes, no shadow of sorrow floating over her beautiful countenance. "My Lord," said she, "Your wife is ready to go wherever you would go." "My darling," replied *Ráma*, "You are bred and born in comforts and luxuries; you cannot, stand the fatigues and difficulties of an ascetic. Remain in *Ayodhyá*." *Sitá* stopped him and said, "You taught me that a wife's paramount duty is to follow her husband in weal or in woe. How could you say otherwise now? I wo'nt hear any refusal." She was determined to follow her husband and would not mind any obstruction. So *Ráma* had to yield and to promise to allow her to follow him.

They took off their royal costumes, and put on the garb of ascetics. Thousands and thousands of people had assembled at the palace-gate to see them, to weep for them and to prevent them from going, if possible. *Ráma* comforted them, assuaged them, bade them all loving and endearing farewells. He came out with his beloved brother and dear wife and the city of *Ayodhyá* wept aloud to see them in ascetic garb. They passed through the weeping mass and entered into the nearest jungle.

[4]

THE poor king *Daçaratha* could not survive the shock; he died as he fainted, never again uttering a word. *Bharata* was not at *Ayodhyá* when all these sad occurrences happened. As soon as he learnt of the sad news,—the news of his father's death and of his brother's banishment,—he hastened to the capital.

He did not speak to his mother; he did not hesitate to express his strong displeasure for her wicked behaviour. He performed his father's funeral ceremony and repaired to the jungle in search of his brothers.

They met; they met in tears. *Bharata* fell at his brother's feet and entreated him to come back to *Ayodhyá*. "Dear brother," said he, "If you do not go,—send *Lakshmana* or send *Satrughna*,—allow me to accompany you." "My beloved brother," replied *Ráma*, "If I go back, our father's promise will not be fulfilled;—could we do this? Go back and govern *Ayodhyá* in my name. I shall return after fourteen years and assume the Government. I entreat you to follow my advice. You know, you are bound to obey your elder brother." "I am bound to obey you," said *Bharata*, "but I won't sit on the throne. Give me your shoes; I shall place them there and they would be your emblem and I shall be your representative."

So this was done. *Bharata* and *Satrughna* returned to *Ayodhyá* ;—*Ráma* with his brother and wife left the forest and proceeded southward visiting many holy places. They came to the seats of many great *Rishis* and by their request drove away the *Rákshasas* from various places.

They at last came to a forest, called *Panchabati*, a beautiful place watered by the river *Godávari*. *Sítá* was enchanted with its silvan scenery ; it was arranged to pass sometime in this Nature's panorama of rivers and trees, foliage and flowers. Huts were made on the bank of the river by the side of a flowery grove. They lived very happily for months amongst singing birds and loving beasts.

Here in this forest *Surpanakhá*, the sister of king *Rávana* used to live with two great *Rákshasas*, named *Khara* and *Dushana*. She one day happened to see *Ráma ;* she at once fell in love with him and offered to marry him. She gradually grew very insolent, when at his brother's order *Lakshmana* cut off her nose and sent her reeling and bleeding to her wild abode. Her piteous cries filled the forest with melancholy echo ; then came *Khara* and *Dushana* in wild fury to punish the princes for the great indignity done to the sister of the *Rákshasa* king.

Ráma went out and gave them battle. Soon they were killed and *Surpanakhá* fled to the island city.

There she narrated before her great brother all that had happened. She wept and prayed for vengeance. *Rávana* had heard from various sources the deeds of *Ráma* and the defeats and retreats of the *Rákshasas*; but he did not think the matter so important as to require his personal interference. He heard much of *Sitá's* beauty; he was tempted,—he thought, he should see what sort of beings these princes of *Ayodhyá* were. He held a private council and finally decided to bring *Sitá* to his golden city. He took with him his uncle *Máricha* and started for the beautiful forest of *Panchabati*.

The *Rákshasas* were great adepts in magic; they could do many wonderful things and assume every possible shape at their will. *Máricha* took the shape of a golden deer and went frolicking before the cottage of the Royal ascetics. *Sitá* asked her husband to catch it and *Ráma* took up his bow and arrows. He came to the deer, but he could not catch it,—it frolicked and played and then fled from him. He pursued it from place to place, till he came very far off his cottage. He got tired in pursuing it; he aimed and shot at it, when the disguised *Rákshasa* fell dead crying, "Oh *Lakshmana*, come and help me." The piercing cry echoed and re-echoed till it filled the whole forest.

The plaintive cry reached *Sitá's* ear; she started and asked *Lakshmana* to go immeditately to the help of her dear husband. But the young prince refused to move. "My Lady," said he, "Do not be anxious for him; he is invincible. This forest is full of *Rákshasas*. It is all their doing. I cannot leave you alone."

Sitá lost her good sense in the apprehension for her dear husband; she got angry and began to abuse poor *Lakshmana*. "Oh you wicked youngman," cried she, "You intend to rob your brother of his kingdom and wife!" "Mother," replied the prince, "You force me to leave you alone. I am not to blame. God protect you." He then drew a circle round the hut and requested her not to come out of it, but to remain quietly in the hut till they would return. He took up his bow and arrows and hastened away.

No sooner he was gone, than *Rávana* in the disguise of an ascetic came to the door of the hut and asked for alms. *Sitá* requested him to wait a little, saying that her husband was out. But the false *Rishi* appeared to be angry for the slight and threatened to go away. There was no greater sin to a Hindu than to allow an ascetic to go away from his door disappointed and displeased. *Sitá* came out and went to the *Rishi* to give him alms. But she was immediately seized and dragged away.

Oh! how she wept; how she struggled; how much she blamed herself for driving away *Lakshmana* from the cottage. Oh! how much she entreated the cruel king to let her go; how many times she fell at his feet and asked for mercy, but all in vain.

[5]

HERE in the deep depth of the forest *Ráma* grew very anxious when he heard the dying cry of the disguised *Rákshasa*. His heart told him that it foreboded some great evil to his dear wife. He apprehended that his young brother might come to his help, leaving *Sitá* all alone. He lost no time, but hastened towards the cottage. But as he feared, he met his brother in the way. "Oh, dear brother," cried *Ráma*, "You have left *Sitá* alone?" "What can I do," replied he, "She forced me to come to your help."

They then ran towards the cottage, as fast as they could. *Ráma* came panting to the door and cried, "*Sitá*, dear *Sitá*, come out and relieve me from my anxiety." None answered,—all was quiet and still. They rushed into the hut, but there was no *Sitá* to be found. They hastened to the bank of the river; they ran to the flowery grove; they searched every creek and corner,—but there was no *Sitá* to be found. All the forest was filled with the heart-rending lamentations of the bereaved husband.

Sitá threw her ornaments all the way, hoping they would tell her husband the direction she had been carried away. They saw these ornaments and went in search of her; but on and on they went and no *Sitá* could be found. They at last came to an old hero,—who had been mortally wounded.* They asked him if he could tell them where their *Sitá* had gone away. "My dear boys," replied the dying hero, "You do not know me, I am a friend of your father; my name is *Jatáyu*. I saw the wicked *Rávana* taking away your wife. I fought with him,—but I am now old. He has defeated me and gone away." He died,—the princes placed him on the funeral pyre and proceeded southward in search of the great city of the *Rákshasas*.

They at last came to a hill, where they saw five big monkeys† of the species that inhabited the great

---

* *Jatáyu* was a very big bird,—brother of *Garura*, whom *Vishnu* rides.

† In the *Rámáyana* these monkeys are described as human beings except that they were monkeys in shape.

kingdom of *Kishkindhá*. They were all rational human beings and perhaps more powerful than men. *Ráma* came to them and asked them "Can you tell me who has taken away my wife ?" "Yes," said one of them, "We have seen the wicked king of *Lanká* taking away a beautiful girl ; she might be your wife. But who are you ? From which place are you coming ?"

Lakshmana told the monkey-hero all about their sad fate. "We are as miserable and unhappy" replied the monkey," as you are. There sits king *Sugriva*, the brother of *Váli*, the great king of *Kishkindhá*. My name is *Hanumán*, I am one of his attendants. King *Váli* has banished us all. If you help us in regaining the kingdom, we can help you in regaining the Princess."

There on the top of the hill the pledge of friendship was taken. *Ráma* promised to kill *Váli* and place *Sugriva* on the throne of *Kishkindhá*. *Sugriva* promised to march out with his monkey-army and recover *Sitá* from the city of *Lanká*.

Poor *Váli* was soon killed and *Sugriva* ascended the throne. He sent his emissaries to the four quarters of the globe to find out the place where *Sitá* had been kept hidden. *Hanumán* went to the south, jumped across the sea and entered the golden city of *Lanká*. He found the city unequalled in beauty, in magnificence and in wealth. He saw the great *Rákshasa*-army and its wonderful array of arms and ammunitions. He saw innumerable horses, countless chariots, and hundreds of elephants. He roamed in disguise all over the city and found the weeping *Sítá* kept as prisoner in the garden of *Açoka*. He was at the point of returning back to *Kishkindhá*, when it struck him, that he should inform the *Rákshasas* that he had honoured their city with his august presence. He began to make himself rather free with the properties of the *Rákshasas* ;—so he was soon caught and brought before the king.

When he was asked who he was, he did not hide the real facts. "Oh wicked king," said he, "I am an ambassador from the court of the great king of *Kishkindhá*. He is coming to *Lanká* in order to help *Ráma*, who is the most powerful king of *Ayodhyá* and whose wife you have stolen. I have been sent to see what sort of a city you possess, so that king *Sugriva* might teach you a lesson."

Rávana got very angry ; he would have ordered the execution of *Hanumán*, but his ministers prevented him from doing it, for an ambassador was never to be killed. But the king ordered the face of the monkey to be burnt and thus disfigured he was to be sent back to his impudent king. In the attempt, *Hanumán* managed to burn half of the golden city ;

he then jumped back to the mainland ; thence he repaired to *Kishkindhá* and told the king the history of his mission.

[6]

A FEW days after, king *Sugriva* marched out with his monkey-army and came as far as the sea. They saw the golden city of *Lanká* floating on the blue ocean like a magnificent piece of gem. They encamped and king *Sugriva* ordered his army to make a bridge over the mighty sea.

Thousands and thousands of monkeys went up the hills and penetrated into the forest ; they brought down stones and trees, and threw them into the sea. By months' incessant labour a bridge was made, the remnant of which is still to be seen and is known as the Adam's Bridge.

The whole monkey-army crossed the sea, encamped before the city and beseized it from all sides. Every precaution was taken to prevent the place from being surprized and stormed.

King *Rávana* had two brothers, named *Kumbhakarna* and *Bibhishana,* the former was a giant and a monster, the latter was virtuous and good. He had a son, named *Indrajit,* who was unequalled in arms and invincible in wars. He had innumerable cousins, countless sons, powerful relatives and able generals; but except *Bibhishana* there was none in *Lanká* who was not an adept in wickedness and sin.

Good and virtuous *Bibhishana* tried to induce his brother *Rávana* to give up *Sitá* and make up the difference; but he was deaf to all reasons. In open court when he entreated the king to give her up,—*Rávana* lost all control over his wild temper; he kicked him and drove him out of the town. *Bibhishana* went to the enemy's camp and we need not say, he was received with open arms.

The great War began; it lasted for ten long years. One after another the sons and cousins, generals and heroes of the great king came out to give battle, but none returned alive. At last *Kumbhakarna* came, but he too did not return from the field of battle. Sad fatality had overtaken the golden city of the sea!

There was only one invincible and all-conquering hero, whom the monkey-army could not defeat. Prince *Indrajit* came out more than once, attacked *Ráma* and his army, defeated him hopelessly and routed his monkey hordes. So long he was alive, *Lanká* was safe and the recovery of *Sitá* was a hopeless task. *Ráma* appealed to his friend *Bibhishana* to save him and his army from the deadly attacks of his invincible nephew. "Dear friend", said *Bibhishana*, "None can kill *Indrajit* if he be in arms,—especially if he comes out to battle, performing his *Pujá*. However, I am at your service and can do every thing for you. Allow *Lakshmana* to accompany me; I shall take him to the place where *Lakshmana* would be able to kill him."

Next day *Lakshmana* and *Bibhishana* entered the city unrecognised. They passed by gate after gate and finally went into the palace of the prince. They passed stealthily into the room where the hero was engaged in prayer. He was soon attacked by the Prince of *Ayodhyá*. He was armless, but he fought like an enraged lion, till he was cut down. They came out of the city in disguise, as they went in, and none knew the foul deed they had committed. There were great rejoicings in the monkey-camp, but soon there were loud lamentations all over the beseized city.

The bereaved and enraged father, the great king of the *Rákshasas*, *Rávana* came out to exterminate *Ráma* and his monkeys from the face of the earth or to die in the field of battle. He was too proud to pray for mercy or to negotiate a treaty. There was terrible carnage on both sides till the evening, when the great king fell and the *Rákshasas* fled precepitously into their ruined city.

Bibhishana was placed on the throne and *Sitá* was brought back in pomp. *Sugriva* went away to

Kishkindhá, but *Hanumán* went with *Ráma* as far as *Ayodhyá*.

* * * *

Poor *Sitá* was never happy. She lived some years in *Ayodhyá*, when *Ráma* banished her into a jungle, because his subjects questioned her chastity; —they thought *Sitá* must have been leading a life of infamy, when she was at *Lanká*. *Ráma* in order to please his people asked *Lakshmana* to take her away from the royal palace and to leave her into a forest. This most unjust and cruel step was taken and *Sitá* was banished for ever.

When *Lakshmana* left her in the jungle, she was some months with child and there at the holy seat of *Rishi Válmiki*, she gave birth to a twin, who were named *Lava* and *Kusha*. They were brought up by the great *Rishi* and were given the education befitting their royal rank.

A few years after, when *Ráma* with his brothers came out to conquer all the chiefs and potentates, the two young princes met them in battle; they defeated them and made them prisoners. The old *Rishi* came and interfered; there was a reconciliation and *Sitá* with her sons returned home full of happiness and bliss.*

* This tale is the briefest narrative of the great Sanskrit epic *Rámáyana*.

THE BATTLE OF KURUKSHETRA.*

[1]

IN the modern province of Delhi there was in ancient time a kingdom, called *Hastinápur*. The Lunar Dynasty held sway over this vast sovereignty. At the time of which we are speaking, king *Sántanu* was the ruling sovereign. He married *Gangá*, and the fruit of this marriage was a son who was named *Vishma*.

---

* One of the biggest sanskrit works is the *Mahábhárata*. It is one of the eighteen great *Puránas*; it can be called an Epie poem at the same time a great history. We can very well glean from it a very clear history of the people of that period. This tale is the briefest narrative of the great battle on which the poem is based.

Once at a time king *Sántanu* went out hunting and in his excursions met a very beautiful daughter of a fisherman, who was called *Satyabati.* He fell in love with her and offered to marry her, but the fisherman did not agree to the *Rájáh's* proposal, till he could promise to bestow the kingdom upon the son of his daughter. King *Sántanu* had already a son, whom he could by no means deprive of his rights. He, therefore, returned home, but felt the disappointment very keenly.

His son *Vishma* marked his father's melancholy mood ; he enquired and learnt of the secret cause of his father's mental sufferings. He determined to make him happy and went to see the fisherman. He promised to relinquish all his claims over the kingdom and not to marry, so that no son could be born to him. He secured *Satyabati,* brought her home and offered her to his father.

Satyabati had a son before her marriage, named *Byása* and now she gave birth to two more sons. One died early, the other was married to the daughter of *Káshi.* But he too died, leaving no heirs. As *Vishma* had taken the vow of celibacy, the great Lunar Dynasty was at the point of becoming extinct Therefore according to the custom of the age, *Satyabati's* illegitimate son *Byása** was invited to

* This *Byása* was the celebrated *Rishi* who compiled the

live with the widowed Princess as her husband.* She gave birth to two sons. The elder became blind and was named *Dhritaráshtra ;* the other was called *Pándu*. Another son was begot by *Byása* on a maid of the Princess and he was called *Vidura*.†

Vishma gave his brothers the highest possible education. As *Dhritaráshtra* was blind, *Pándu* was declared to be the Heir-Apparent; but *Vishma* promised to take special care of the blind Prince and never to desert him and his children. When they grew up *Dhritaráshtra* was married to *Gándhári,* the Princess of *Gándhár* and *Pándu* was married first to the adopted daughter of king *Kunta* of *Bhoja* and then to *Mádri,* the Princess of *Madra*.

---

four *Vedas* and wrote eighteen great *Puránas*. In fact all great Works are supposed to have been written and compiled by him. He is one of the most celebrated *Rishis* of ancient India.

* All through this tale readers would find laxity of the marriage system and want of female chastity.—It is evident, in those days the morals in India were quite different from those that of the modern world.

† It is said that when the widowed princess went to *Byása* she found him so very fearful that she shut her eyes. Thus the son that was born to her became blind. Next time she gathered courage and kept her eyes open, but turned very pale,—so her son that was born became *Pándu* which means pale. On the third time when she was asked to go to *Vyása*, she did not go at all, but sent one of her maids.

Princess *Kunti* before her marriage with *Pándu* gave birth to a son, who was named *Karna*. In course of time another son was born to her and he was named *Yudhisthira*. Then *Gándhári* gave birth to one hundred sons* successively and *Kunti* two more. *Mádri* gave birth to a twin and king *Pándu* died. The other two sons of *Kunti* were named *Bhima* and *Arjuna*, and the twins were called *Nakula* and *Sahadeva*. The eldest son of *Gándhári* was called *Duryyodhana* and another out of the rest was named *Duswashana*. They were all placed under the tuition of a very learned Brahmin, called *Drona*, who had a son named *Aswathámá*.

[2]

Yudhisthira was very virtuous and gentle, *Bhima* was physically a giant ; *Arjuna* grew up as the best warrior. *Duryyodhana* was as strong as *Bhima*, but he grew up very vicious and wicked.

* There is an anecdote in connection with the birth of the hundred sons of *Gándhári*. It is said that when she was told that *Kunti* had given birth to a son, she was mortally sorry, because her son would never be a king. She forced an abortion and tried to destroy the embryo and cut it into a hundred pieces. But finally she repented and wept for her mad conduct. A great *Rishi's* assistance was sought for and he put life into these hundred pieces, making one a son.

All his brothers imitated him in his wicked ways and grew up as bad as he was. *Aswathámá* and *Karna* were also brought up with these Princes, the former became fond of luxuries, the latter however became a great warrior. *Karna* and *Duryyodhana* gradually became fast friends.

Yudhisthira was the eldest son of the late king *Pándu*; he was also the eldest of all the brothers; therefore in course of time he was declared to be the Heir-apparent. The sons of *Dhritaráshtra* were known as *Kurus* and those of *Pándu* as *Pándavas*. The *Pándavas* were good and gentle and they were very much liked by the people. The *Kurus* were bad and wicked and the people were afraid of them. The people of *Hastinápura* were happy to learn that good and virtuous *Yudhisthira* would be their future king. But wicked *Duryyodhana* could not bear the sight of his brother's glory. He began to device plans to humiliate the *Pándavas*; he was backed by all his brothers and his maternal uncle *Sakuni* plied him with evil advices. It was finally arranged to murder the five *Pándavas*.

They were tempted to go to a place called *Váranábata*, where *Duryyodhana* caused a house to be built. It was made of materials which could easily ignite. It was secretly arranged to burn the *Pándavas* in this infernal house. They knew nothing of the evil intentions of their cousins; they came to live in this house with their mother. But *Vidura* loved them more than his own children; he privately informed them of the nature of their danger.

The *Pándavas* then held a consultation. "Dear brothers," said *Yudhisthira,* "if we go back to *Hastinápura, Duryyodhana* will know that we have learnt his evil designs. The army and the treasury are in his hands,—the chief men of the *Durbar* are all on his side. If we go back, surely he will attack us. We shall be easily defeated and perhaps killed. My advice is to fly from this house. Let us travel all over the country *incognito* and try to make friends with other kings and princes. When we shall feel ourselves strong to fight with the *Kurus,* we shall come back and demand our kingdom." To other brothers the words of the eldest were commands; they agreed to go wherever he went.

One day at the dead of night they set fire to the house and fled from the place. People thought that they must have been burnt to death.

[3.]

THE *Pándavas* assumed the garb of ascetics and roamed about for months. *Bhima* met with an aboriginal girl in the jungle and married her. A son was born to this marriage and was named *Ghatotkacha*.

They at last left the jungle and came to a country called *Panchál.* There they learnt that the king *Drupada* had taken a vow of giving away his daughter to the warrior who would be able to shoot the target which he had constructed. It was a wonderful piece of mechanism. The target was placed on a very high pole and a golden fish was placed behind it. There was only a very small bore in the target, through which one of the eyes of the golden fish could be seen. The warrior would have to hit the fish seeing its reflection in water, which had been kept underneath the target.

Many princes from many places had come to secure the beautiful damsel and to show their feats of arms. *Vishma, Drona, Karna, Duryyodhana* and all the other princes and warriors of *Hastinápura* had also come to this great tournament. One after another the princes tried to win the damsel, but none could hit the eye of the fish. Then rose *Vishma.* "I have taken," said he, "A vow of celibacy and therefore cannot marry the Princess. If however I be successful, my nephew *Duryyodhana* will have the girl." He took up the bow, but saw before him *Shikhandi,* the son of king *Drupada,* who was an eunuch. To see an eunuch was an evil omen and *Vishma* never used to take arms on seeing an evil omen. He silently left the bow and came back to his seat.

Then king *Drupada* cried, "Of whatever caste or creed one might be,—whoever would be able to hit the fish I shall give away my daughter to him." Then rose *Drona*. "If I win the Princess," said he, "I shall give her to my pupil, *Duryyodhana*." He took up the bow, aimed and sent up the arrow, but failed to hit the golden fish. Then rose *Karna* amidst the cheerings of the *Kurus*. "If I can hit the fish" said he, "The Princess would go to my friend *Duryyodhana*." He tried but he too failed.*

The Princes of *Pándu* went to the assembly in the garb of Brahmins ; they were sitting amongst the mendicants who had come for alms. But *Arjuna* grew impatient to rise and shoot,—he was eagerly looking at his brother to get his permission.

Again and again cried king *Drupada*, "Kings or beggars, Brahmins or Sudras, whoever he might be,

* It is said that when *Karna* and *Drona* shot at the fish *Krishna* who was present and who knew that the *Pándu* Princess were present in disguise put his *Sudarsana Chakra* over the target and thus prevented their arrows from going up to the fish, *Sudarsana Chakra* is the weapon of *Vishnu*. All through the *Mahábhárata Krishna* had been represented as the incarnation of the great Preserver. *Krishna* wanted the princess to be won by his friend *Arjuna*.

let him come and try to shoot at the fish. My *Draupadi* would surely go to the successful man."

Finding that every one had failed and *Arjuna* was eager to accomplish this wonderful feat of arms, *Yudhisthira* at last gave him permission to go and try his chance. He rose amidst the titterings of the Brahmins and hisses of the Princes. He appeared to be the poorest of the poor, but he slowly and silently went to the target and looked towards the great assembly. He bowed first to *Drona,* his tutor and then to *Vishma,* his grandfather. Both of them were astonished to find a beggarly Brahmin bowing to them, for they knew *Arjuna* to be dead. Then he took up the bow, saw the reflection of the fish on the water and sent up the arrow. It went up like a flash of lighting and hit the fish amidst the loud cheerings of the Brahmins. The Princes could not believe that such wonderful feat was possible of a poor Brahmin and they made a great noise. However it was finally decided that he had really won the Princess.

[4]

THE *Pándavas* with beautiful *Draupadi* returned home in the evening. "Mother," cried *Bhima* from the door, "We have got something grand to-day." "My sons," replied she, "Partake of it all brothers." To obey their mother's command they all married the Princess and it was arranged,—to avoid future disagreement,—that when one of the brothers would be with her, no other brother would go to her or to the room where she would be. If any of them would violate this rule, he would be bound to go to banishment for certain years.

King *Drupada* soon came to learn that the five poor Brahmins were the five Princes of *Pándu* in disguise. He brought them home in all honour and pomp ; the news flew from place to place like wildfire and it soon reached *Hastinápura*.

King *Dhritaráshtra* under advice from *Vishma* sent *Vidura* to bring them back to the capital. They all came back and lived in a new city, called *Indraprastha*, separate from *Duryyodhana* and his brothers. There they lived happily for months.

One day a poor Brahmin came to *Arjuna* and piteously appealed to him to rescue his property from robbers. Unfortunately *Arjuna's* arms were in the room where *Yudhisthira* was with *Draupadi*. To save the poor man's property he faced the dread penalty of banishment. He went into the room, took up his arms and hastened to help the poor man.

After chastising the robbers he returned to his brothers and asked their permission to go to banishment. With very sorrowful heart the brothers bade him farewell and *Arjuna* left *Indraprastha* and went out on pilgrimage.

He travelled all over the country and at last came to *Pravásha.* His dearest friend *Krishna,* the king of *Mathurá* and *Dwáraká,* went to meet him. He brought him to his capital and gave his sister *Subhadrá* in marriage with him. Here he passed many a happy day with his friend and wife.

We need not say that he met with many adventures in his travels It is superfluous to mention that he showed many wonderful feats of arms in helping the needy and punishing the wicked.

After the completion of the specified time for banishment, he came back to *Indraprastha* and joined his brothers. They all lived very happily, and they tried their best to please the *Kurus* by every possible means.

Duryyodhana married Princess *Bhánumati* and several children were born to her. Their daughter *Lakshmaná* fell in love with the son of *Krishna.* The young couple were married in great pomp, both branches of the great Lunar House taking prominent parts in celebrating the nuptials.

[5]

Bhima, Arjuna, Nakula and *Sahadeva* went out according to the custom of the age to conquer the adjacent kingdoms. They subjugated many kings and exacted tributes from various principalities. They returned home with hoard of wealth and Raja *Yudhisthira* celebrated the victory by holding the *Rájsuya Yagma.* It was a grand and magnificent Durbar, in which numerous kings and princes came to pay homage to the great *Pándavas.* All was joy and merriment; everyone was happy, except *Duryyodhana* and his brothers. They could not bear the success of the *Pándavas;* the glory and the happiness of the Princes of *Pándu* were gall and worm-wood to them. They returned to *Hastinápura* resolving upon taking vengence.

They held a secret council, in which uncle *Sakuni* adviced them to invite *Yudhisthira* to play. "A *Kshatrya*," said he, "Can never refuse to accept a challenge when asked to fight or to gamble. I shall play dice with him and win all his property and wealth. Let us disgrace them before the whole world."

The wicked advice was accepted; king *Yudhisthira* was invited to play; and the most unfortunate game was begun. It was a great gambling match,—the *Pándavas* were on one side and the *Kurus* on the other. The place was the great Durbar hall and the audience was the whole *Hastinápura.*

Fortune was against the Prince of *Pándu;* he began to lose. He gradually lost all his wealth,—he lost all his possessions, his palaces, horses and elephants. He was up in the play ;—finding that he had nothing else to bet, he betted his younger brother and lost. He then one after another lost all his brothers. He then betted himself and lost too. There was nothing more to lose ; he raised up his head, looked round that great assembly and wiped away the hot drops that had gathered over his forehead. "*Yudhisthira,*" sneered *Sakuni,* "Bet this time *Draupadi,* your wife. You are sure to win, for she is a lucky woman." He silently began to play and betted his dear wife ; but fortune was terribly against him, he lost again.

There was great glee on the side of the *Kurus* ; they again and again cheered for their victory.

Wicked *Duryyodhana* was mad with joy. "Oh friends!" exclaimed he, "These *Pándavas* are now our servants. Let them sit with the menials." *Bhima* could hardly control his anger,—*Arjuna* was trying to calm him. Young *Nakula* and *Sahadeva* were piteously looking at their eldest brother, enquiring what they were to do. But *Yudhisthira* calmly rose from his throne, majestically walked towards the servants and sat with them. His obedient and loving brothers all rose up with him and went to sit with him amongst the menials.

Duryyodhana was not satified with thus humiliating his own cousins. He ordered his brother *Duswáshana* to go and bring *Draupadi* and make her a maid-servant. The daughter of a king and the queen of the great *Pándavas* was dragged out of her appartments and brought before the Durbar. The whole *Hastinápura* wept and the people cried "Shame."

Draupadi stood before the people and wept aloud. She appealed to all present to save her from this disgrace; but none came to her rescue. At last the youngest brother of *Duryyodhana*, feeling pity for her, rose and said, "*Draupadi* cannot be made a maid-servant, for cousin *Yudhisthira* lost him first and then he betted her." "When *Yudhisthira*," replied *Duryyodhana*, "Lost all his property, he must have lost his wife with it. Let him say, that it is not so and we shall give up our claim over *Draupadi*."

Bhima could not control himself any longer; he snatched himself away from the grasp of *Arjuna* and rose. "You scoundrels," roared he, "I would have thrashed you out of your existence,but I control myself for the sake of our most beloved brother. Raja *Yudhisthira* is the Lord of all the world. In his victory the whole world is conquered and in his loss the whole world is lost;—what you speak of *Draupadi* or of a dozen of us !"

[6]

AT this point good *Vidura* interfered ; he went first to *Vishma* and then to king *Dhritaráshtra.* He told the blind monarch what his wicked sons had done. He entreated him to save the *Kurus* from the wrath of the *Pándavas* and to protect the great Lunar Dynasty from the self-dissension and self-destruction. The king brought the *Pándavas* to him and freed them from their eternal slavery. They were allowed to go and to begin life anew.

Duryyodhana was much disappointed. He could not disobey his father's command and could not prevent the *Pándavas* to go away. But he knew that it would be very easy for them to conquer fresh kingdoms and to secure wealth untold. He called his uncle *Sakuni* to advice him what to do and how to destroy these thorns in his path to glory.

"Invite them again," said *Sakuni,* "To play and ask them to bet in this wise. If they lose, they will have to go to the jungle for twelve years, the last year of which they shall have to pass *incognito.* If they are found out, they will have to go again for 12 years and so on. We are sure to find them out and rest assured they will never be able to come back." "Dear uncle," replied *Duryyodhana,*"suppose *Yudhisthira* declines to play or to go to the jungle at all!" *Sakuni* smiled and said, "My dear nephew you do not know *Yudhisthira*".

Next morning *Yudhisthira* was again challenged to play. His brothers entreatingly asked him not to accept the challenge, but *Yudhisthira* replied, "Dear brothers, do you advice me to neglect the holy duties of a *Kshatriya!* God has destined us for misery; let us calmly submit to His will".

The unfortunate play was again begun, and again *Yudhisthira* lost the game. They sacrificed themselves for virtue and truth and silently left *Hastinápura* to pass 12 years in banishment. Their faithful and dear wife *Draupadi* followed them to be the partner of her husbands' miseries, and amidst the wails of the people they entered into a deep forest.

There they lived like ascetics for eleven years; at last the time came when they had to live *incognito*. It was a very difficult task to them, for they knew that the *Kurus* would move heaven and earth to find them out.

One night they left their jungle-abode and went to the kingdom of *Birát* in disguise. There *Yudhisthira* giving himself out as a dice-player, became the Raja's companion. *Bhima* became his cook; *Arjuna* assumed the garb of a female and calling himself an eunuch* became the dancing and

* It is said that *Arjuna* when in banishment went to heaven

music master of the princess *Uttará*, the daughter of the king. *Nakula* became the horse-keeper and *Shahadeb* the shepherd. Poor *Draupadi* entered the service of the queen as one of her maids. There they lived very quietly and happily for a year and the *Kurus*, notwithstanding all efforts, failed to know their whereabouts.

A year passed. *Duryyodhana* in his depredatory excursions came into the *Birát* country. King *Birát* went out to give him battle; but the *Kurus* by a manuœver eluded him and looted his kine. The queen asked his son *Uttara* to go and save them, but he was a boasting coward. "*Mámá*," said he, "If I had a good charioteer, I would have gone and taught a lesson to the thieving *Kurus*." The Pseudo-maid of the queen said that the music master of the princess was a very good charioteer and would surely go with the prince, if asked by the queen. She immediately ordered him to come to her and when he came, she requested him to go with her son.

Arjuna took the prince in his chariot before the *Kuru* army. The timid young man attempted to

---

to learn the art of arms. *Indra* in his honour sent the heavenly songstress *Tilotyama* to him, but *Arjuna* declined to accept her. She took offence and cursed him,saying that he would be an eunuch for a year. Thus when *Arjuna* became the music master of the young princess of *Biráta*, he was really an eunuch.

fly from the chariot, when he found that to fight with the *Kurus* was not a child's play. *Arjuna* prevented him from leaving the field, gave him his real name and promised to rescue his kine. He then went to a tree where he had kept his arms hidden. He took them down, armed himself and hastened to attack the enemy. The *Kurus* were soon routed and they fled in hot haste towards their own capital.

King *Birát* found out the disguise of *Yudhisthira* and his brothers. He placed him on his throne and gave the *Pándavas* all possible honour. His daughter *Uttará* was married to *Abhimanyu*, the son of *Arjuna*, his mother being *Subhadrá*.

[8]

THE news very soon reached the capital of the *Kurus*. The blind king *Dhritaráshtra,* the Nestor of the Lunar House, *Vishma,* the great preceptor, *Drona,* the good and honest *Vidura,* all tried to induce *Duryyodhana* to make an amicable settlement with the *Pándavas,* but he at the advice of his evil-making uncle *Shakuni* and his ambitious friend *Karna* put a deaf ear to all their good advices. *Krishna,* the friend and relative of both the parties came to mediate. "*Duryyodhana,*" entreated he, "Give the five brothers only five villages of your vast domain. They would be satisfied with the smallest, that you will offer them." "No, not an inch of land", replied he, "Without a mortal struggle".

So battle was determined upon on both sides. Both parties sent out invitations to the allied kings and princes. Great preparations were made for the coming struggle and soldiers were collected from every part of the Empire.

Krishna was the greatest man of the age.* Both the contending parties were eager to secure him, but to him both parties were equally dear and near. When appealed to, he said that he could not take arms against any of them, but he would be present in the battle with him who would come to him first. *Duryyodhana* hastened to *Dwáraka* and went to meet him, but he found him asleep. There was a golden throne near the head of *Krishna* ; he sat on it and patiently waited till he would rise. A few minutes after *Arjuna* came and sat at his feet. *Krishna* opening his eyes saw *Arjuna* and asked him what he could do for him. "I have come, said he, "Oh friend, to pray for a gift." "What can I give you my friend?" replied *Krishna*. "You know that I am always at your service." "Give me," said *Arjuna*, "Your goodself. I want nothing else." *Krishna* smiled and replied, "My

* Read *Srikrishna*.

dear friend, you must have heard that I have resolved not to take arms in this battle. What help it would be to you to get me ?" "Dear friend," said *Arjuna*, "I know I shall win the battle, but I shall not be happy if my dearest friend be not a partner of my glory and happiness." "Very well," said he, "I shall be your charioteer."*

He turned his head and saw *Duryyodhana*. "Dear brother," said he, "You have heard what I had told *Arjuna*. However, I am bound to serve you. Would you like to have me or my invincible army ?" *Duryyodhana* thought it would be useless to take *Krishna* who would not fight. As for council he would get better from his dear uncle *Shakuni*. It was surely something to get *Krishna's* great army. He said, "I shall thank you, Oh brother, if you will kindly give me your army." *Krishna* agreed and *Duryyodhana* returned to *Hastinápura* with the invincible army. Then *Arjuna* left *Dwáraka* and *Krishna* accompanied him.

When all preparations were complete *Yudhisthira* marched out with his army and encamped on the field of *Kurukshetra*.† *Duryyodhana* with his

---

* We need not say that all this was pre-arranged by *Srikrishna* and was a ruse to king *Duryyodhana*.

† The field of *Kurukshetra* is considered to be one of the

stupendous army came out of *Hastinápura* to give him battle.

[9.]

THERE were millions of soldiers* on both sides; the greatest generals and the most powerful potentates had come to meet in mortal struggle. It was a battle between brothers and brothers and friends and friends. On one side there were the greatest of the great *Vishma,* the ablest of the able *Drona,* the bravest of the brave *Karna.* There were hundred sons and numerous grandsons of the blind king, backed by the most powerful chiefs of India. On the other there were the five Princes of *Pándu* with their sons *Abhimanyu* and *Ghatotkacha.* There were king *Drupada* and king *Biráta* and some other kings and princes, connected with them either by blood or by marriage. And to crown all there was *Krishna* who was their guide, friend and leader.

Vishma had promised never to desert the children of the blind king. With the greatest sorrow and regret he consented to command the *Kuru*-army

---

Hindu pilgrimages. It is situated in the Punjab, some miles off from Delhi by Delhi-Kalka Railway.

† It is said that there were altogether 18 *Akshauhinis* of soldiers on both sides. An *Akshauhini* is equal to ten millions.

for ten days. It was useless to try to describe his feats of arms, for there was none so great, either in war or in council. He killed almost the half of the *Pándava*-army.

The *Pándavas* held a council of war. "Friends," said *Krishna*, "None in the world can defeat *Vishma*, so long he will be in arms. Accept my advice,—there is nothing bad or nothing good in this world, for this world is mere an erroneous dream of the Soul.* Do your duty;—your duty is to win the battle and don't mind the means. *Arjuna*, do thou take *Shikhandi* with you to-morrow. *Vishma* will surely leave off arms if he sees him. That is the opportunity,—defeat him, overpower him, kill, if necessary and save the *Pándava* army."

Next day *Krishna's* advice was adopted. *Vishma* saw *Shikhandi* on *Arjuna's* chariot. He smiled and left arms. Immediately *Arjuna* mortally wounded him and great *Vhisma* fell frcm his chariot. The leaders of both parties hastened to the wounded Patriarch. Both the *Kuru* and *Pándu* princes wept bitterly for him, for surely he was more than a father to them all.

The next day the *Kurus* came out to give battle under the command of *Drona*. He arranged his

* Read *Gitá* in the appendix.

army in a most wonderful array. The *Pándavas* found that it was impossible to break the enemy's line, or to penetrate into the semi-circle formed. But young *Abhimanyu* by his most daring charge broke into the circle and killed many thousands of the enemy. But he was soon hemmed in by the *Kurus*. Seven great warriors such as *Drona* and *Karna* rushed upon him in wild fury. The poor boy was soon overpowered and killed. *Bhima* rushed to his rescue, but before he could reach the young hero, he fell mortally wounded from his chariot. *Bhima* became ten times furious by grief and vengeance. He killed thirty of his wicked cousins, and felled a thousand of the enemy.

On the other part of the field Raja *Drupada* fell and *Karna* killed *Ghatotkacha.* Every where the *Pândavas* were defeated and routed. *Arjuna* when fighting with *Drona* was mortally wounded and he fainted on his chariot. Then *Krishna* cried "Oh *Drona*, your son is killed." Really an elephant named *Aswathámá* was killed by *Bhima*; but *Krishna* gave out that *Aswathámá*, the son of *Drona*, was killed. The old warrior was overwhelmed with grief on hearing his beloved son's death. But he did not and could not believe that *Aswathámá* could be killed. "Oh *Krishna*," said he, "I cannot believe that my most beloved son is dead. Let

Yudhisthira say that my son is no more and I shall believe it, for I know he cannot tell a lie."

Krishna managed to bring *Yudhisthira* to the great warrior; he asked him to say that *Aswathámá* was dead, but *Yudhisthira* positively refused to tell such a falsehood. But *Krishna* was up to anything; he finally induced him to say "*Aswathámá* is dead, the elephant." When *Yudhisthira* said "The elephant," *Krishna* blew his great conch and the words did not reach *Drona's* ears. When he was told that his son was dead, he fainted and immediately one of the warriors on the *Pándava* side jumped upon his chariot and cut off his head.

[10]

THE next day, *Kurus* came out under the command of *Karna*. There was hand to hand fight from morning to evening. Blood flowed like water and reddened the field of *Kurukshetra*. *Bhima* killed *Duswáshana* and the rest of his wicked cousins, but he had to retreat having been defeated by *Karna*. Many fell on both sides, and the *Pándava* army was gradually driven back and finally routed. *Arjuna* soon came to rally round his army, and stood face to face with *Karna*. Both were equally great in arms; they faught like lions for hours together till *Karna* fell. The *Pándavas* cheered lustily and the *Kurus* retired to their camp.

Early next morning the *Pándavas* attacked the *Kurus* with renewed vigour. Raja *Biráta* fell fighting, but the most wicked *Sakuni* was killed. The whole *Kuru* army was disorganised and by evening they were hopelessly defeated and routed, and the *Pándavas* were in hot pursuit.

It was soon rumoured that Raja *Duryyodhana* had fled from the field. The *Pándavas* immediately pursued and found him hidden in a place of safety. When he saw that there was no escape, he came out and challenged *Bhima* to single combat. They faught like two mad elephants,but king *Duryyodhana* at last fell mortally wounded.*

The *Pándava*-army retired to their camp. They were all tired and exhausted and knowing their victory sure they fell asleep. At the dead of night *Aswathámá* came to the wounded king and promised him to bring the heads of the *Pándu* Princes.

He stealthily entered the *Pándava* camp ; he

* Every part of king *Duryyodhana's* body except the thigh was as hard as iron. No weapon could have any effect on any part of his body. *Bhima* in the heat of the fight forgot that he was to hit *Duryyodhana* on his thigh ; but *Krishna* was there. As if encouraging *Bhima*, he repeatedly clapped on his own thigh. The hint was soon understood and king *Duryyodhana* was mortally wounded.

went into the tent, in which *Draupadi* was asleep with her five young sons. He gagged them, he killed them one after another and hastened with their heads to the dying king. But *Duryyodhana* perceived the mistake committed by the son of *Drona*. "My friend," faultered he; "You have killed the last scions of the Lunar House." With these words on his lips the poor king breathed his last.

The *Pándavas* came to *Hastinápura* after the victory. But it was a victory saturated with the blood of all that was dear and near to them. There was no joy ; there was no merriment. Their entrance to the capital of their forefathers was not ushered in by the sounds of drums or the boomings of fire-works. Slowly and silently they entered the palace, but there were heart-rending lamentations all around.

* * * *

THE five Princes of *Pándu* lived for some years and at last they retired into the jungle to pass the remainder of their lives in prayers and meditations.

Princess *Uttará*, the wife of poor *Abhimanyu*, was with child, when her husband fell on the field of battle. She gave birth to a son, who was named *Parikshit*.

When Prince *Parikshit* grew up, he became the king of *Hastinápura*.

NALA AND DAMAYANTI.

[1]

AMONGST all the great and good monarchs that flourished in ancient India, none was equal to king *Nala* of *Naisadha*. In greatness, in piety and in philanthrophy, he stood towering over all. He treated his subjects as his own children,—the poor of his kingdom were the members of his own royal household. The gods were worshipped and the Brahmins were honoured in every house all over his vast dominion. Happiness, comfort and ease were to be seen everywhere ; misery had fled from the land over which benign king *Nala* had his kind sovereignty. His wife *Damayanti* was equally good. Her mind was full of human kindness ; in her mind was all that was holy and celestial ; nay she was the mother of the people of *Naisadha*.

But in this world where nothing is permanent, but all is transitory and fleeting,—king *Nala's* and queen *Damayanti's* happiness did not last long. *Kali* the God of sin* had an eye over them from a long time,—but so virtuous were the king and the queen that he did not get an opportunity to wreck his vengeance upon the happy pair.

At last one day he found *Nala* engaged in worship not with the prescribed ablution ; he forthwith got possession of his mind and led him to evil ways.

He became very much fond of dice ; he threw himself madly into the whirlpool of gambling ;—he began to neglect his royal duties,—he was slowly drifted into the wide gulf of vice and sin. He gambled with a cousin and gradually lost all his possessions ; *Kali* made him a beggar and drove him out of his happy home and his smiling capital. His loving wife *Damayanti* followed him as a shadow follows its substance ; uncomplainingly and ungrudgingly the royal queen walked by the side of her

* *Shani* and *Kali* are supposed to be two very powerful gods. We have given two tales in which it has been shown that these gods of evils shower on the head of an unhappy man all sorts of miseries.

husband and left behind her all that was dear and near to her. They had no other possessions but the two pieces of clothes that they had on their person; and they were shunned by all that used to love them before.

Driven by the evil God they fled on and on, till they entered into a deep forest. There they rested, thoroughly exhausted and broken down. They had not touched food since three days,—hunger was at their back and starvation in front. Good king *Nala* was not at all sorry for his change of fortune,—for he was strong enough to endure it; but alas! how could he bear the great sufferings that his most beloved wife had to undergo! Though she was smiling,—though she was very happy by her husband's side,—yet to king *Nala* it was gull and wormwood.

They rested underneath a tree, till king *Nala* saw a golden bird merrily dancing near at hand. The bird might fetch some money, if sold in the market. The money might keep them up for sometime. *Nala* at once stood up and tried to catch it by throwing over it his cloth,—but alas, the bird was the God of evil in disguise. It took up the cloth and flew away-living the poor king in a state of nudity. It had not satisfied the wicked God by reducing a great king to a state of most deplorable misery; still he was at his back ; still his fearful vengeance had not been fully wrecked upon the king ; still he wanted to make them more and more miserable.

[2]

WHEN night came, *Nala* and *Damayanti*, putting round their loins only one cloth that they possessed between them, tried to pass the night in the forest as best as they could. *Damayanti* was tired and exhausted,—she soon fell into a deep sleep.

But the poor and the unhappy king could not sleep ;—thought after thought, most painful, rushed into his mind and made his wakeful night most miserable. He was not sorry for himself ;—he could bear no longer the sufferings of his beloved wife. *Kali* entered into his mind and whispered into his ear, "Leave her,—why make her miserable ?" Indeed, why should she be made miserable for his misfortune ? She was the queen of a vast province,—she was the daughter of a most powerful king. Why should she be made a partner of his misery ? If she had not been allowed to accompany him,—she would have gone to her father's kingdom and there lived happily till he could join her.

But how to part ? She loved him so much that it would be impossible for him to snatch away from her loving grasp. She was asleep ;—he could very well fly from her,—but half of the cloth was round her loins ; he could not go in a state of nudity. The wicked God who took possession of his mind again plied him with evil advices ;—he cut the cloth half and half ; he silently rose from her side and left poor *Damayanti* alone and unprotected there in that great forest at the dead of night. He fled ;—he fled like a mad man far far away from his most beloved wife.

Damayanti awoke and did not find her husband by her side ; she found herself alone in the midst of wild beasts,—as far as her eyes could see she found nothing but deep forest of trees entwined with fantastic creepers. She wept,—her loud lamentations filled the place with sorrow,—she again and again cried for her husband and appealed to him to come and save her from danger,—but who would hear her lamentations ?—*Nala* had fled,—fled many miles from his loving wife.

We shall not attempt to describe the pain and misery of unhappy *Damayanti*. She had to meet insult, misery, starvation at every step till she came to the kingdom of *Chedi*. The mother of the king saw her pass by the street ; she took compassion upon her ; seeing the most miserable plight in which she was, she at once despatched a maid to bring her into the palace.

There *Damayanti* lived as a companion to the royal princess ;—if she was not happy,—she could not be on account of her husband's absence,—she was beyond the insults of the vicious world. She lived in *Chedi* for years,—but heard no news of her absent husband.

[3]

WHEN king of *Bidharva,* the father of queen *Damayanti,* learnt of the state of affairs at his son-in-law's kingdom he hastened to *Naisadha.* But he found them not ; he was told that they had left their kingdom and had entered into the jungle. He made a searching enquiry all over the kingdom,—but could get no trace of his unhappy daughter. He returned to his capital and sent emissaries all over the country to search for his daughter and for the good and the great king *Nala.* His men journeyed some in disguise and some in state ; they went to all the surrounding kingdoms and searched every creek and corner,—but almost all came back baffled in their attempts. No news was received of the unhappy king and the queen.

At last one of the emissaries named *Sudeva* came to *Chedi* and lived there in disguise. He met *Damayanti* in the palace and although she was living like an ordinary maid he at once recognised her to be their missing princess. He appeared in the royal court and told the king that the maid was no other than their beautiful *Damayanti*, the queen of *Naisadha* and the Princess of *Bidharva*. Now the queen of *Chedi* was the sister of *Damayanti's* mother; she was beside herself with joy to learn that the maid, whom she loved, was no other than her own sister's daughter.

Damayanti passed some days with her royal relatives in great joy; then she asked them to allow her to go to her father's kingdom where her children whom she had sent to her mother, were living. The king and the queen of *Chedi* sent *Damayanti* with *Sudeva* in a way befitting her high rank.

We need not say that she was received with open arms by her parents. There in *Bidharva* she lived for years, wistfully looking for the return of her beloved husband; for she knew the evil influences of *Kali* could not last for more than some years.

But she did not rest quiet;—she made her father send again emissaries all over the country in search of her husband. She told them to enquire for him at every village and ask every man the following question. "What justification was there for a man to leave his wife behind clad in half of the cloth?"

All returned without any information,—but one came back with a reply. He had gone to the kingdom of the king *Rituparna* and there met his charioteer, named *Báhuka*. He put the question to him as ordered by the princess and the following was the answer given by the charioteer. "If one's husband does an act most condemnable, the wife should hide it instead of giving it out to the world."

Damayanti suspected this charioteer to be her husband in disguise. He asked *Sudeva* to go at once to the capital of king *Rituparna* and inform him that she was again going to be married. *Sudeva* was to bring the king and his charioteer by any means to the capital of *Bidharva*. Clever and intelligent *Sudeva* started for the court of king *Rituparna* and soon reached his kingdom.

[4]

We must now say what happened to the unhappy king after parting with his dear wife.

He hastened away from the forest, lest his wife did come and follow him. He ran at his utmost speed to quit her and to be at a great distance from her. But on his way he met a snake and found it in great distress. His kindness rose above all other feelings; he took it up and tried to save it, but the ungrateful reptile bit him, and he was at once disfigured.

To him the evil turned to be a good; for now none could recognise him as the king,—he was so very much disfigured that perhaps his own dear *Damayanti* would not have been able to recognize him.

He passed through many countries, unknown and uncared of; he at last came to the kingdom of the king *Rituparna*; and learning that the king wanted a charioteer he offered himself for the post. His services were accepted, for none there was so efficient in driving as he. Here in the service of king *Rituparna* he lived for some years till *Sudeva* appeared in the court of the king and announced the marriage of Princess *Damayanti*.

King *Rituparna*, learning that there would be a *Sayambara*,* grew eager to go to the capital of *Bidharva*, so that he might be present in the assembly from which the beautiful princess would make her choice. He ordered his charioteer *Báhuka* to get his royal chariot ready as soon as possible, for he would at once start for the kingdom of *Bidharva*.

So he started for the *Sayambara* with his charioteer who was no other than king *Nala* himself

Sayambara* is an assembly in which a princess makes her own choice of a bridegroom from the assembled people.

in disguise. They reached the kingdom of *Bidharva* in due time and king *Rituparna* was received by the king in all honour. But there was no *Sayambara,*—for it was mere a trick of *Damayanti* to bring her husband to her father's capital.

As soon as the king arrived, *Damayanti* sent one of her maids to the king in disguise. We need not say that very soon the mystery was divulged; king *Nala* was recognized. He was taken to the royal court and a most cordial reception was accorded to him by the king and his subjects.

The wicked god of evil, *Kali,* finding that his time had expired, fled from the body of the king. *Damayanti* and her husband came to their own kingdom; the king of *Bidharva* came to place them on the throne with a powerful army at his back. The usurper fled in dismay and king *Nala* and queen *Damayanti* were again very happy.*

* *Kali* is in fact the period of Time that is supposed to be full of vice and sin. The entire Space of Time is divided into four parts namely *Satya*, *Tretá*, *Dvápara*, and *Kali.* Here in this tale *Kali* is the god of Sin and vice. The moral of the tale is apparent; the virtuous and the good, as soon as they are touched by *Kali*, *i. e.* by vice and sin, lose all and become most miserable like king *Nala.*

SRIBATSA AND CHINTA.

[1]

THERE once arose a great dispute between the goddess *Lakshmi* and the god *Shani*. *Lakshmi* is the goddess of wealth ; he, on whom she casts her benign eyes, becomes the richest of the rich ; his treasury is filled with all the wealth of the world ;—luxury and plenty rolls over his vast mansion. But *Shani* is the god of poverty and misery ;—he, on whom this fearful god throws the fiery glare of his scorching eyes,—becomes the poorest of the poor ; his home turns to be a desert where misery and want take pleasure to dance and play.

Both were powerful in their own way,—but proud *Shani* sneered at the beautiful goddess and vaunted that he was the greatest of all the gods ;—his power was far greater than that of the goddess of wealth ; nay he could ruin a man on whom *Lakshmi* would shower her favours. "Brother *Shani*, replied the goddess, "What is the good of mere vaunting. We both rule over the destiny of men. Let us go and ask one of them whether you or I am considered to be the greatest of the gods." *Shani* consented ; and *Sribatsa*, the most powerful, the richest and the noblest of the kings then living, was selected by them as the fittest man to whom to go and put the question.

They both appeared in his royal court and were received by the king in all honour. "Oh king" said the fearful god, "Tell us whether—*Lakshmi* or I am the greater of the two." Good king *Sribatsa* knew not what to say ;—surely who is there in this world who does not know *Lakshmi* to be the greatest and the best of all the goddesses ? Who does not know that *Shani* is the most hated ? But king *Sribatsa* was afraid to offend the angry god. He most humbly prayed to them to allow him time to answer their question. He most respectfully asked them to come again next day, when he would reply to their query.

He placed a golden throne on his right and a silver one on his left. When the god and the goddess appeared in his court he stood up and requested them to take their seats. *Shani* walked up and sat on the silver throne,—*Lakshmi* in her own majesty sat on the golden one. Then the king sat upon his throne and addressing the fearful god thus said, "Oh god, you can now judge yourself who is the greater of the two. You have sat on the silver throne which is placed on my left. You know that a golden throne placed on the right is more honourable than the throne on which you have thought fit to take your seat."

The fearful god's anger knew no bounds; he left the court of king *Sribatsa* resolving upon taking vengeance. He vowed to show something of his great power;—he determined to see how the goddess of wealth could save him from his terrible anger.

[2]

POOR king *Sribatsa* fell, and the benign goddess *Lakshmi* could not save him from the fearful vengeance of the god of evil. *Shani* took possession of his destiny and drove away the goddess of wealth from his door. "My dear son," said she when parting with king *Sribatsa*, "I have been forced to leave you,—but I shall be always by you. *Shani* will not be able to rule over your destiny very long. I shall soon come back again and make you happy and prosperous." "Mother," replied the king, "let the evil god ruin me,—but still I consider you the greatest and the best of all the gods."

By the evil influences of *Shani* the prosperous and happy kingdom of king *Sribatsa* was run over with plague, famine and internal strifes. Fields were left untilled and jungle grew up all around ;—the houses crumbled down for want of repairs, villages were taken possession of by the wild beasts ; rivers and wells were dried up, and towns became high mounds of ruins. What had been once a happy and prosperous kingdom, became a barren and depopulated desert.

King *Sribatsa* asked his wife *Chintá* to fly from the palace and to go to her father's kingdom,—but she refused to leave her husband. She resolved to follow him in weal or in woe. Finding her resolute, king *Sribatsa* asked her to take all her jewels in a bundle and to follow him, for he had determined to leave his plague-stricken kingdom. At the dead of night they left their capital and fled from the land which had been taken for his own by the fearful *Shani*, the god of all evils. They fled and ran as fast as they could, to leave a place where death and misery were dancing in their demonaic merriments.

They came to the side of a great river and found an old man sitting on a broken boat. There was no other boat to take them across the river so they determined to cross in that dilapidated boat and to utilize the services of the old man· "Yes," said he, "I can take you on the other side of the river,—but my boat will not stand more than the weight of one man. You better wait, give me the bundle I shall reach it first,—then I shall one by one take you two on the other bank of the river." The king consented and put the bundle which contained all the earthly wealth of theirs on the broken boat of the old man ; but as soon as it was placed on the boat,—the old man, the boat, the river, all vanished from their sight. The king and the queen came to know, that it was the work of *Shani*,—so they soon left the place hoping to get rid of the evil influences of the god.

They had not any food for two days,—so the great king, who used to distribute alms freely, had to beg for his food and ask for alms of some fishermen, who were fishing in a small streamlet. They gave him a fish and as they had nothing else to dress and cook it, queen *Chintá* collected some woods, made a fire and burnt the fish. But it grew so blackened that the queen knew not how to place it before her husband. She thought to clean it and went to the streamlet to have it washed. But alas, as soon as she placed it into the water,—it flew away from her hand, dived down and disappeared into the water.

The poor queen could not control her feelings and burst out into tears. The king hastened to his beloved wife and when he learnt of what had happened, he asked the queen to leave the place at once,—for the evil god was there.

[3]

THEY came at last to a. village, inhabited by wood-cutters ; the king and the queen found the place very quiet and comfortable,—just the place where they could live happily, if not in luxury and affluence. The king made friends with the poor men, the queen by her loving conduct drew all the women towards her. Thus they became the objects of love of the simple but honest wood-cutters,—and the king with his beloved queen, lived in that village as one of them.

Thus they passed many days ;—at last one day, a rich merchant passed in a boat along the river that rolled by the side of the village of the wood-cutters. The boat struck the ground and notwithstanding all efforts of the merchant and his men it did not move. It was all the doing of the god of evil ; he appeared before the merchant as a Brahmin astrologer. "Oh good Sir," said the disguised god, "There is a woman called *Chintá* in this village,—if she touches your boat, it will move. Nothing else will be able to move it." The merchant hastened to the hut in which the unhappy queen used to live. He appealed to her to come to her rescue. He prayed for her kindness. The men were out in wood-cutting,—the king was also absent,—*Chintá* was unwilling to go without the permision of her husband. But the women were much moved by the piteous appeal of the merchant; they pressed her to go and help the man in his difficulty if that was possible by her. On account of the importunities of her neighbours, she at last agreed to go and accompanied the merchant to his boat. As soon as she got on board the boat, it moved and floated down the river. The ungrateful merchant determined to force the queen to accompany him; for he thought if she were in his boat, there would be no future danger. Thus *Chintá* was not allowed to come down, but was forcibly carried away.

When the king returned home, he learnt that his wife was gone. "Oh god of evil," cried he, "At last you are victorious. You have stolen from my side my goddess of happiness and bliss." He left the village and went in search of his missing wife.

He travelled all over the country, but he found nowhere any trace of his beloved queen. He was told that a merchant in a boat had taken away his wife,—he went down the river,—walking all along the bank. He scrutinized every boat that passed, but found not his darling wife.

At last he came to the kingdom of *Báhu*, a chieftain of great power and wealth. He had a most charming daughter named, *Bhodrá*,—for whom the king had declared a *Shayambara* and had sent invitations to all the chiefs and potentates. King *Sribatsa*, although he was living as a poor wood-cutter, thought of attending the great assembly in which the beautiful princess would make her choice of a husband.

He was not allowed a seat,—but he stood near the assembly underneath a tree. The princess came and stood before the great assembly,—she saw the princes in their jewelled garb and in their royal array;—she scrutinized each and every one of them,—but she passed them all and came straight to the place where the disguised wood-cutter was standing. She took the garland of flowers which was round her neck and placed it round that of king *Sribatsa*.

There were titterings and hissings all over the assembly;—king *Báhu* felt himself terribly humiliated; but he could not prevent his daughter from making her own choice of a husband. He ordered his ministers to provide the princess and her husband with all the necessaries of life,—but they would never be allowed to enter the palace again.

[4]

THE princess left her father's palace and went away with the wood-cutter, whom she had thought fit to make her husband. They lived in a house in the suburb of the city and were provided with all that they wanted to make them comfortable and happy.

But king *Sribatsa* was not happy. He could not be possibly happy without his beloved wife *Chintá* by his side. He knew that the Goddess of wealth was always taking care of him and providing him with happiness and comfort,—he knew that the fearful God *Shani* would have to leave him soon; he knew, he would get back his loving wife and his happy kingdom;—knowing full well all that would happen, he could not be happy without his beloved *Chintá*. He sent men to watch every river and to search every boat; he sent emissaries all over the country with the promise of handsome rewards; he himself often rode out to see if he could find her out.

At last his men caught hold of a boat and prevented the merchant to proceed further. King *Sribatsa* was informed and he hastened to the boat.

Yes, it was the very merchant who forcibly carried away the poor queen,—it was the very boat in which she was kept a prisoner. The king confiscated all the property of the wicked man and ordered his men to search the boat in order to find his beloved queen. The man ran to king *Báhu* and prayed for protection ; the king called for his son-in-law and when he appeared in his royal court, he asked for an explanation.

King *Sribatsa* then told him all about his sad history;—he told him how the wicked man carried away his queen and how he had kept her prisoner in his boat.

King *Báhu*, with all his retinue accompanied by king *Sribatsa*, went to the merchant's boat. There they found the unhappy queen pale and haggard in the hold of the boat, hand and foot bound in chains. The queen was soon made free and was taken to the palace in great pomp. There were joy and merriment all over the city ;—king *Báhu* made every possible arrangement to give the king and the queen a grand reception, befiitting their high rank.

King *Sribatsa* passed a few days in the capital of king *Báhu* and then he proceeded to his own kingdom accompanied by his two loving wives.

The God of evil, *Shani*, left them and their kingdom; there were again prosperity and happiness in the vast domain over which the good king ruled. *Lakshmi*, the goddess of wealth, again smiled over the land and graced the place where she used to reign, till the fatal day, when she quarrelled with the God of misery and was driven out of the land by his fearful and vindictive temper*

* The moral of |this tale is apparent. Both happiness and misery, wealth and poverty, with equal power rule over the destiny of man. The preceding tale shows that vice and sin bring a man to the lowest depth of misery,—but in this tale it is shown that even very good and virtuous man often suffers the pangs of misery and wants of poverty out of the unknowable laws of Providence who has made the gods of prosperity and poverty equally powerful and strong, with the full and equal authority on both to rule over the destiny of man.

PRAHLADA.

[1]

THERE were in ancient time two great tyrants, named *Hiranyakshya* and *Hiranyakashyapu*, who conquered almost whole of India. They trampled down all the established institutions and sneered at the name of religion. Vice and sin were their favourites ; debauchery and carnality were their fond pastimes ; men were the objects of their cruelty and the gods were those of their hatred.

The bitterest hatred and the deadliest enmity they bore for the great Preserver, *Vishnu*. They would always wage war against him ;—they would wreck their severest vengeance upon those who were his worshippers; the temples of *Vishnu* were blown off and his idols were desecrated by the *Chandálas.** Religion and society, *Yagma* and *pujah,*—all were destroyed under the regime of the two wicked brothers.

But unknowable are the ways of Providence. *Hiranyakshya* was killed when he went to fight with the gods and the germ of the poison which would kill *Hiranyakashyapu* grew in the birth of his own son. This boy was named *Prahláda.* None was so good as he. He was the incarnation of all that was good in creation;—kindness, benevolence, affection, love were his ruling feelings; he was a thorough contrast of his great but wicked father.

He was placed under a tutor with instructions to teach him hatred towards all that was virtuous and good. He was to learn all sorts of wickedness; he was to be taught all the intricate ways of vice and sin. He should bear the bitterest hatred towards the God of Preservation and the deadliest enmity towards all his worshippers. But alas,—the boy was made of a different metal. He refused to learn anything else but that which was good and virtuous; he openly declared his love for *Vishnu* and his worshippers. He not only refused to be bad, but asked his tutor to mend his evil ways and taught his play-mates to be

* *Chandálas* are the lowest and the most degraded caste.

good and kind and to love the great God who was the fountain-spring of all good and who so kindly ruled and preserved the great universe.

The tutor upbarided him, chastised him, bat him,—but to no effect. The days of wickedness were gone and the goodness flourished everywhere. Vice and Sin fled, giving place to virtue and love. The tutor was alarmed; he knew not what to do; the king would be awfully offended and he was fully aware that his head would be severed for the obstinacy of the young prince. Finding no other means of saving himself from the wrath of the great king, the poor tutor went to the king, fell upon his knees and told him all that had happened. The king frowned,—all the court trembled; the tutor fainted out of fear. But the king pardoned him and ordered a man to bring the prince to his royal presence.

[2]

Prahláda came; and does ever goodness fear the frowns of evil? He stood calm and majestic, proud and great; his sublime countenance and lovely appearance drew reverence from all those that were present. The great king's heart shook as the prince majestically walked up and stood before his royal throne.

"*Prahláda,*" began the king, "I am told that you disobey your tutor; you mind not his lessons. You love *Vishnu* and worship him who is my greatest enemy. Perhaps you do not know that I and my people hate *Vishnu* with all their heart. Go, boy, behave properly and never utter the name of *Vishnu.*" "Father," said the young prince, "*Vishnu* is the source of all good; *Hari** is all love. How can I forget him?" The king was terribly provoked; none ever dared utter the name of *Vishnu* before him. His own son not only utters but praises his greatest enemy before his very face! His face became like a burning furnace; his eyes rolled like fire-balls, his hairs stood on their end. "Ungrateful boy," roared he, "I pardon you for your impudence, because you are my son, but beware of my anger. Be careful to mend your ways. If I again hear that you have uttered the name of that god for whom I bear the bitterest hatred, you will not escape,—no, your life will not be worth a feather."

The Prince retired, the court dissolved and the king went in great anger to complain to his queen against the outrageous conduct of his wicked son. She brought the prince before him, kissed him, carressed him and then entreated him to give up *Vishnu*-worship. "My darling boy," said the queen,

* *Hari* is another name of *Vishnu.*

"Do not offend your father. He is very choleric. He can do everything, if he loses his temper." "Dear mother," replied the boy, "how can you ask me to do it? Should I be wicked and vicious? Is not *Hari* the god of love? Is he not the source of all good, all happiness, all bliss?" The young prince threw his tiny hands round his mother's neck and said, "Mother, mother dear, do not mind the wicked words of my father. He has gone astray;—he has sold his soul to the god of evil. Mother, hear me, love my loving *Hari*, he will give you eternal bliss." The mother again and again kissed her dear son, and said, "Dear *Prahláda*, you do not know your father; he is a fearful man. Be careful not to utter these words before him."

But the Prince had tasted the ambrosia that makes man imortal; he had tasted the unknowable bliss of heavenly love that is the living source of the universe; he had tasted that which is heavenly. How could he control himself? His heart was full,—his feelings were uncontrollable,—he not only drank deep the spring of eternal love, but he began to distribute heavenly bliss to all that came to him. He sang the sweet name of *Hari* and he danced at the name of his God of love. Soon the city was filled with the song of *Hari*;—every house became the seat of his worship;—every man and woman threw himself at the feet of the great God *Vishnu* for salvation and for eternal bliss.

The great king's anger knew no bounds; he ordered the guards to hasten and to bring the prince before him in irons. He held a council of his ministers and told them that the boy must be killed, for if he be allowed to grow up, it would be impossible to stop him from spreading mischief through out the kingdom. They agreed and the executioners were called in.

The Prince was brought and placed before the royal throne. "Foolish and arrogant boy," roared the king, "Did I not order you to desist from uttering the pernicious name of *Vishnu?*" The young prince fell on his knees and said, "Father, *Hari* is the God of love. Pray for his eternal love and you will be blessed." The king rose up in an indomitable rage." Take away the boy," roared he, "Kill him this instant." The prince was dragged away.

[3]

A GREAT fire was made and the virtuous and the good prince was thrown into that all-devouring element. *Prahláda* clasped his tiny hands and prayed, "Oh my loving *Hari*,—save me." He stood into the blazing fire, but not a hair of his head was scorched.

The executioners took him on the top of the nearest mountain and threw him hand and foot bound into the deepest abyss. The young prince uttered the name of *Hari* and leaped into the yawning gulf below. He came down upon the earth, but not a scratch was made upon his body.

He was then dragged away to a place where there were many wild and mad elephants. He was thrown before these fearful beasts to be trodden under their huge feet. But, lo! they came fawning at him, played and danced round him and at last one of them raised him up with its trunk and placed him on its back.

The executioners took him away and threw him into the cage where snakes of the deadliest type were kept, but even they,—the servilest of the poisonous kingdom,—did not touch him.

They despaired of his death,—but they were afraid of the king. They did not dare inform him that they had failed in executing the condemned prince. They sharpened their swords and tried to behead him,—they adopted a thousand and one means to kill the young prince, but all in vain. The Prince had been saved by Him who preserves the smallest thing of the universe. Who could destroy him whom the God of love takes on His loving breast?

The king was at last informed. He was astonished; he was bewildered; he knew not what to do. He finally ordered the prince to be brought before him.

Prahláda came and stood before his father. The king stared at him,—but the prince shivered not before his fiery eyes. He stood, as only good and virtuous men could stand before the god of evil. The king staggered at his majesty of demeanour; for the first time in his life he felt in his mind the shiverings of fear. He asked the prince to come near him and to tell him who had protected him from death. "Dear father," said the prince, "the God of all gods,—the Preserver of all preserved,—the fountain Spring of all Life, the good and the loving *Vishnu*, whom I love and worship,has protected me." "Is he so powerful," asked the king, "that he can protect you from my fearful wrath?" "Oh father," replied *Prahláda*, "Why do you ask me of his power? He, who rules over the universe, who is the *Cause* of all that we see and perceive, is Almighty and Omnipotent."

"Where does he live?"

"He is every where; He is Omniscient and Omnipresent."

The king could not control himself any longer; he stood up in wild rage, and striking the pillar that stood by his throne roared. "Tell me, Oh arrogant boy, does your *Hari* exist in this pillar?" The boy knelt down, raised up his loving eyes towards the heaven and said, "Yes father, when He is every where, he must be here in this pillar too."

The king immediately took up a heavy club and struck the pillar with all the strength of a giant. The pillar trembled from top to bottom and then fell down in a heap. There issued from the pillar a fearful monster,—his body being that of a man and his head that of a lion.* It advanced towards the king and took him up on his lap, as if he were a child. The king struggled, he roard, he foamed,—he rolled in mortal pain, but all in vain. The monster thrust its fearful claws into the stomach of the wicked tyrant and rent it into parts. He was torn into pieces and flung off the throne, from which he spread vice and sin all over the land.

Prahláda prayed on his knees;—he knew that his loving God had at last appeared to rid the world of the wicked and vicious. The God smiled and disappeared.

---

* This appearance of *Vishnu* is considered to be one of his incarnations. *Vishnu* is said to have ten incarnations, namely Fish, Turttle, Boar, Human, Lion—(the one in this tale), Dwarf, *Parasurám*, (who exterminated the vicious *Khastryas* 24 times), *Ráma*, *Sreekrishna*, *Budha* and *Kalki*. The last has not as yet taken birth. He will come as a warrior on the back of a fiery steed and clear the world of all the wicked and vicious.

THE LOST RING.

[1]

KING *Dushmanta* was one of the celebrated rulers of ancient India. His victorious standard was honoured in every part of the country ; under his benign sway the people were very happy and prosperous.

Once on a time he went out hunting and lost himself in the deep forest. He left his retinue far behind and came alone and unattended to the holy seat of *Rishi Karna*. It was an oasis in a desert,—it was a most charming garden in that great forest. Beautiful flowers were spreading their sweet fragrance all over the place and gliding creepers with their many coloured flowers were shedding their lusture on this Nature's Panorama. All was beauty and sublimity. The king was charmed to see the place and he advanced to enjoy it. But what did he see,—was it real or visionary ? Were they angels of heaven or creatures of the earth ?

He saw three beautiful damsels watering the flowery plants ;—one of them was exquisitely beautiful ; her beauty was not of this world ; the imagination of the greatest poet and the finest painter could not reach her charms. Her companions were addressing her by the name of *Shakuntalá*.*

She was the adopted daughter of *Rishi Karna* ;† she was a wild flower budded and blossomed in the solitude of forest and asceticism. She had not seen this world of care and struggle ;—she had not seen the field where vice and sin fight with virtue

* Perhaps we need not say that the drama of the above name is the best in the Sanskrit language ; it is supposed to be one of the best dramas of the world. The original tale from which the great poet *Kálidása* wrote his drama is in the *Mahábhárata*. This drama has been now translated into all European Languages.

† It is said that *Shakuntalá* is the daughter of the celebrated *Rishi Viswámitra*,—her mother being *Manoká*, a songstress of heaven. When she was born, *Manoká* left her in the forest, for she could not take a human being into the celestial region. But she told *Rishi Karna* all about the history of the girl and asked him to bring her up.

and goodness for supremacy ;—she was all simplicity and innocence.

She was young and full of that beauty and grace which was beyond the power of all description. Her rising breasts, her flashing cheeks, her rosy lips, her healthy look reflected the blossoming mind and heart, that were incased in that charming temple of Beauty. The flowery plants were her children,—the birds and beasts were her companions ; she lived in Nature and Nature lived in her.*

The king found her watering the lovely plants ; he never saw such beauty in all his life ;—her beauty was imprinted on his loving heart and her charms thrilled through his every nerve. He stood behind a tree and continued to see her ; if he saw her till the end of his life, his thirst for seeing her would not have been satiated.

A buzzing bee† came flying at her and tried to sit upon her most charming face. Perhaps the poor innocent thing took that face for a smiling lily. She tried to drive it away, but it flew round and round and attempted to sit again. She, having been much troubled and bothered, entreated her friends to come to her rescue. But they were enjoying at her embar-

* The readers should mark the similarity of *Kâlidâsa's Shakuntalâ* with Shakespear's *Miranda* (Tempest).

† The exact insect was *Bhramara,* which is not a bee.

rassment. "Dear *Shakuntalá*," said one, "How can we help you out of your difficulty? The ruler of all this domain is king *Dushmanta*. Pray to him to come and grant you protection."

The king found this to be a very good opportunity and excuse to appear before the ladies. He came up to *Shakuntalá* and said, "Who asked protection from me? I am here present." The ladies were joking at their friend; they never expected to see the real king. They were taken aback, they were ashamed, they knew not what to do and say. But the king by his graciousness and courtesy revived into them confidence and courage; they were soon all talking, as if they were old friends.

[2]

It was no wonder that *Shakuntalá* would fall in love with *Dushmanta*. She never saw such a beautiful human shape,—so graceful, so majestic, so bold and proud; her lot was to see her old father *Karna* with his wrinkled face, his cumbrous hair, his hoarse voice and grave countenance.* Her mind was just blossoming; she was just at that period of

* Here again the similarity of *Shakuntalá* and *Miranda* is very much apparent. *Miranda* saw only her old father Prospero,—so did *Shakuntalá* her father *Karna*.

life when all the feelings grow keen,—when the mind hankers after enfolding some one into its loving bossom. She fell in love with the king,—and knew not why.

The king was already in love. Who could help loving *Shakuntalá ?* When two such loving hearts eagerly desire to unite, who could prevent them from doing it. They were married in the *Gandharva** way. Their love was the love of Nature and their marriage was also the marriage of Nature. There were no ceremonies, no rites, no formalities observed ;—no relatives were present and no friends invited. They met in a sylvan grove,—flowers and folliage adorned their marriage altar and birds sang the bridal music ; Nature herself blessed their nuptial couch. Oh, how happy were they ? King *Dushmanta* lost himself in the whirlpool of love and its concomitant bliss ; he forgot that he had a kingdom with heavy responsibilities ; he forgot that he had come to hunt and had left his friends and relatives in the camp outside. What fault was there

* There are various sorts of marriage systems, chiefly eight, amongst the Hindus. The marriage in which no formal ceremony is held and in which two lovers privately or before only a few of their selected friends exchange garlands of flowers and call themselves husband and wife, is called the *Gandharva*. Amongst the modern Hindus such marriages are not recognised. Such conduct is rather condemned as immoral.

then of poor *Shakuntalá*? She was the impersonation of simplicity and innocence; she never tasted the intoxicating liquor of love and romance; surely she was happy before,—but she never knew what pleasures really meant. She was unconsciously carried away,—where she did not know. Her father was absent from home;—her companions, instead of putting obstruction to her pleasures, helped her in the matter. She drank deep the eternal spring of love.

They passed a few days in their own sweet company;—day and night they were both together like two loving doves cooing in the deepest recess of a bushy tree. Then king *Dushmanta* remembered that he had to go back to his kingdom. But how would he bid adieu to one who never knew what parting meant. To *Shakuntalá* there was no outside world,—she never felt that there was an external world except her dear lover and her sweet self. She thought that the pleasures, in which she had been deeply drowned, would last till the end of her life. But alas, *Dushmanta's* life was not a poetic romance, it was not all imagination;—there were realities,—hard and painful realities in his care-worn life.

So king *Dushmanta* had to part with his beloved *Shakuntalá*; he tried to make the moment as less painful as lay in his power. He removed one of his best rings form his finger and put it on that of *Shakuntalá*. "My darling," said he " as soon as I shall reach my capital, I shall send men to take you there. You will be my chief queen ;—every thing that I posses will be yours." *Shakuntalá* did not understand all that he said; but this much she understood that her lover would leave her for some time and she must allow him to go, notwithstanding the great pain that she felt in doing it. She never knew that love produces so much pain. She felt that her days of happiness were over and the days of tears had come.

[3]

King *Dushmanta* was gone. What a change had come over her? Her birds were not taken care of, her flowers were neglected; the creepers were not cared for, the plants were not watered. Every thing had been changed in that lovely bower; its life had been snatched away.

Shakuntalá was brooding over something; she was always absent. Her mind had flown away to that distant city, whereto her lover had repaired. Elasticity of her character was gone; the girlish sprightliness of her rising youth had disappeared. She had lost her heart and her mind had followed the path of the man who made her so happy.

One day she was sitting at the door of her father's cottage, when the fearful *Rishi Durbáshá** came to her and told her that he intended to be her guest. Again and again the *Rishi* called her, but his words did not reach her ears. She was so absent in mind that she could not hear what the great *Rishi* was telling her. He took offence. "Arrogant girl," said he, "You dare niglect *Durbáshá* in the thought of others ! He, whom you think and for whom you pine, shall forget and neglect you."

The angry words of the fearful *Rishi* fell like thunder; they reached the ears of her companions. They came and fell at his feet; they wept, they prayed,they entreated him to forgive poor *Shakuntalá*. She too had become fully conscious of her position ; she fell on her knees and prayed for forgiveness. The ill-tempered *Rishi* was at last moved. "Well," said he, "My words cannot be retracted. However, show him some token and he will be able to recognise you." *Shakuntalá* had the ring of the king on her finger; there was a token, so there was no cause for anxiety.

But days passed, and none came from the king to take her away. She pined and pined and like a

* *Durbásha* was a great *Rishi*, notorious for his hot and angry temper.

torn flower faded away. Her broken-heart knew no consolation ; she was so miserable!

Her father on returning from pilgrimage was told what had happened in his absence. He was not sorry to learn that his beloved *Shakuntalá* had been married to the great king. He thought it proper however to send her to her royal husband without any further delay, for he knew the ways of kings. He was afraid lest by long separation the king might forget the poor girl of the forest.

He sent her to the king and two of his pupils were despatched to escort her to the city of *Hastinápura.** What silent pleasure did she feel in the deep depth of her loving heart,when she started to meet her lover ?—but how sorry was she to part with her beloved companions, with all that was dear and near to her! What a great struggle it was to her to cut herself off from all her early associations. She bade farewell to all and left the holy seat of her most beloved father in tears. Her companions kissed her and wept upon her breasts ; her favourite birds and beasts looked wildly at her, not knowing what had happened.

Yes, she was gone. The beauty, the Majesty, the Life of the forest was gone. The wild forest-

* King *Dushmanta* belonged to the Solar Dynasty, whose capital was *Hastinápura*. See the Battle of *Kurukshetra*.

flower had been despatched to the city in order to be transplanted in the royal garden. The simplicity and the innocence of Nature had been sent to be mixed up with the vice and sin of the world.

They all came to a river and *Shakuntalá* went to bathe. Fortune was against her ; as ill-luck would have it, the ring, that had been presented to her by her loving husband, slipped off her finger and was lost in the water. How eagerly and with what palpitating heart she searched for it, but alas, all her efforts were in vain ! She did not tell the young *Rishis* what had happened ; she fondly hoped that he, who loved her with all his heart, could by no means forget her.

They came to the city of *Hastinápura*. The young *Rishis* took her to the royal court and presented her to the great king. Poor *Shakuntalá* never saw such royal grandeur ; she never appeared before so many noblemen and warriors ; she trembled like an Aspen leaf.

"Oh great king," said the young *Rishis*, "We have brought with us *Shakuntalá*, whom you were so kind to marry when you graced our holy seat. She is the adopted daughter of our preceptor, the celebrated *Rishi Karna*. Do kindly receive your wife and permit us to go back to our forest-home." The king was astonished, the courtiers looked at one another, the assembled people eagerly tried to see the daughter of the great *Rishi*. The king knew not what to say; he frowned, he felt himself offended,—but by no means he could utter angry words to those who wore the holy garb of asceticism. "Reverend sir," replied he "I am really astonished to hear what you have been pleased to say. I do not remember that I ever married any body lately. I am sorry to say that the lady, whom you have been pleased to call my wife, was never addressed by me. This is the first time I see her in my life. Perhaps something is wrong with her brains." The young *Rishis* felt themselves very much insulted; they prevented the king from proceeding further and said, "King, know that we never speak false-hood. You are no better than a knave to entice a poor girl and to take advantage of her inocence and simplicity."

Poor *Shakuntalá* with superhuman effort kept her feelings down. "Brothers" said she to the young *Rishis*, "Let us leave this place and go back. You need not reprove the king. I know it is all my destiny." "We have suffered enough insult," said one in anger, "For your foolishness and stupidty." "Come" said the other, "to remain any longer in this place is sin." They left the royal court and went back to their forest home.*

* We need not say that the strange conduct of the king was the result of *Rishi Durbáshá's* curse.

Shakuntalá went back broken-hearted. All her hopes disappeared,—the days of her happiness were over.

She gave birth to a lovely boy,—and he was named *Damanaka*. The boy was her only joy in her life of misery and despair.

None was so spirited and bold as young *Damanaka*; every inch of him indicated his royal birth. When he was only six years of age he would run after the cubs of tigers and lions and bring them to play with.

He was the joy of all the *Rishis*; he was the beauty of all the forest. The *Rishis* gave him the education befitting a great prince; he grew up to be a great scholar, a great statesman and a great warrior.

But many years rolled away and king *Dushmanta* never enquired of poor *Shakuntalá*. She pined away in the solitude of wilderness,—in brooding over her own misery and disappointment.

At last the ring was found. A fish devoured the ring when it fell from the finger of the unhappy *Shakuntalá*. But it was soon caught by a fisherman who found it in its stomach. It was a very valuable piece of jewellery;—it was a ring which could adorn only the fingers of royal potentates. Thus when the poor fisherman went to a jeweller to sell it, he was handed over to officials and was arrested as a thief. He was brought before the royal court; he was placed before the great king to receive sentence; he was asked to explain how he had got the ring.

The king saw the ring. No sooner he had cast his glance on that fatal ring, than he grew pale and stunned. The sad tale of *Shakuntalá* flashed into his mind; he remembered everything,—he remembered poor *Shakuntalá* with all her great love,—he remembered that he had married her, he remembered that he had driven her away from his royal presence. Hundreds of poisonous darts went piercing into his heart;—his great love for her returned with hundredfold vehemence;—remorse stang him to the very quick.

He ordered the fisherman to be at once released,—he dissolved his royal court,—he ordered that immediate preparation should be made for him to go to the holy seat of *Rishi Karna.*

He encamped just outside the forest and went alone in search of his missing love. He came near the holy-seat of the great *Rishi;*—there had been much change. The flowery plants had grown wild for the want of loving care of *Shakuntalá;* the beauty and grace, that he saw when he met her in this lovely bower, were all gone.

But he saw something strange. He found a boy playing near the *Rishi's* cottage and dragging mercilessly a young tiger from one corner to the other. He never saw such a lovely and spirited boy; his heart longed to take him upon his lap and caress him.

He advanced and came to him. The boy finding a stranger near gave up the tiger and looked at him. "My lovely boy," said the king, "What is your name? Who is the happy man whom you call your father?" "My name is *Dámanaka*," replied the boy, "I do not know my father's name. He is a wicked man and does not love my mother."

The king's heart palpitated; his blood ran quicker and his voice faltered when he asked, "Who is your mother, my child?" "There is my mother coming," said the boy and ran towards the door of the cottage from which issued a lady.

Shakuntalá saw the king and stood like a statue. She could not advance a step,—she could not utter a word. He came near her and asked forgiveness for his past conduct. He went on to explain the reason of his strange conduct,—but poor *Shakuntalá* fainted.

We need not add that king *Dushmanta* took his wife with him to his capital. There were joy and merriment all over the kingdom. She was given a reception befitting the queen of *Hastinápura.*

Her son was named *Bharata,* and was recognized and honoured as the crown-prince* of the royal house ; and *Shakuntalá* was very very happy.

---

* It is said that from the name of this prince India derived the name of *Bháratabarsha.*

THE BOY DEVOTEE.

[1]

KING *Uttyánapada* had two wives, namely *Suruchi* and *Suniti*. The former was the most favourite wife of the king and the latter was consequently very much neglected by him. *Suruchi* had a son, named *Uttyama* and *Suniti* a son called *Dhruva*.* One day the king was caressing the son of his favourite boy when *Dhruva* was standing by. He was about five years

---

* In a previous tale named *Prahláda*, readers have found a boy in whom devotion and love of God intuitively manifested themselves; but in this tale they would find a boy who gets them by incessant meditation and fervent prayers.

of age. He grew anxious to get on his father's lap and to be caressed by him as he was doing his brother *Uttyama*. But his step-mother was present;—the king, though willing, dared not caress the son of his other wife. He asked him not to come to him, but to go to his mother. "Boy," said the favourite queen, "Do not aspire to sit on the royal throne or to go to your royal father, because you are not born of me. Know your position and behave accordingly. Your mother is no better than a beggarly woman and you are a beggar's brat." *Dhruva*, was mere a boy, but he felt the insult keenly; he went straight to his mother, fell on her breast and wept. "My darling dear," said *Suniti*, "Tell me who has made you weep. Who has become so hard-hearted as to bring tears into your eyes?" *Dhruva* in broken voice and half-suppressed sobs told his mother what had happened and what her step-mother had said. "My poor boy," replied his mother, "Pray to God and and he will give you a position higher than that of all the kings of the world." "Mother," said the boy, "I must get at this high position by my own exertion. Tell me how to get it." "Well my boy," said *Suniti*, "What can I advice you? Pray to *Hari**—and He can make you the Lord of the Creation."

---

* *Hari* is one of the names of God; generally it means *Vishnu*.

The boy left her mother and went out. He became pensive and roamed about the town. He met *Nárada* on the way and asked him where he could go and get *Hari*. The great *Rishi* was astonished to find the most important question about the Soul in the lips of a boy, five years old. He questioned him and learnt all that had happened in the palace, and the great determination that the boy had formed in his mind. "My dear boy," said the *Rishi*, "If you want to see *Hari*, go into the deepest forest and there in fervent prayers ask him to come to you. He is sure to come, for *Hari* cannot remain aloof from His devotees and lovers."

Dhruva came back home and told his mother that he had resolved to leave the palace and enter into the forest, so that he might in solitude pray to *Hari*, to come to him. *Suniti*, finding the boy resolute, accompanied him. One day at the dead of night they left the city and went into a very deep forest. There the royal queen made a hut out of leaves and *Dhruva* went out to pray.

[2]

It was a deep forest, abounding in trees, plants, creepers and bushes. Branches had co-mingled with branches; creepers had been entwining creepers; hardly the rays of the sun could penetrate into that Nature's Botanical Panorama. Beautiful birds were singing the music of heaven and wild beasts were roaring like thunders of the sky. Not a human soul was to be seen any where,—not a trace of any habitation, where man could get protection or shelter.

In this fearful forest, amongst wild beasts and poisonous reptiles, boy *Dhruva* stood kneeling underneath a tree. His hands were clasped, his eyes were shut, his mind was bent on fervent prayers,—prayers to great *Hari* to come to him and to bless him with his loving grace.

Days passed and he prayed and prayed, clasping his tiny hands and raising up his tearful eyes towards the blue expanse over his head. Day and night,—continually for days together he prayed and prayed, but alas, none came to respond to his heart-felt prayers. Lions walked round and round him, wagging their tales and licking their tongues ; tigers crouched and stared at him, but dared not come near him, deadly snakes slided past ; fearful reptiles rolled round him,—but there the boy stood, unmoved and unconscious of all that lay around him. "*Hari,*" cried the boy, "Oh my lotus-eyed beautiful *Hari,* come and let me see you."

How long could the great God of Love withstand the call of such a loving boy ? How long He could remain in Heaven without coming to such a devotee? He came and manifested himself before *Dhruva*.*

He blessed him and asked him why he was praying to him and what he wanted. "Oh my *Hari*," replied the boy, "Make me something which is far higher than the kings and sovereigns of this world." "Well, my darling boy," said the Heavenly Voice. "Is that all you want? Your prayer is granted."

Rishi Nárada came to king *Uttyánapada* and told him all that his son *Dhruva* had done. He told the king that God had appeared to him for his exemplary devotion and love; He had blessed him with his celestial grace;—He had made him a being far more higher than any man living." "Oh king," said the *Rishi*, "Your house has been honoured and glorified by the birth of *Dhruva*. Go, hasten to the forest and honour him. The world is blessed by the birth of such a devotee."

The king and the queen with all the court came to the forest where *Suniti* was living in her poor hut. They embraced the boy, they repeatedly begged his pardon for their previous ill-treatment to him; they kissed him and fell at his feet and cried, "Do thou bless us, thy blessings are the same as those of loving *Hari*, for thou art his most beloved."

* It is mentioned that God appeared before *Dhruva* in his *Vishnu* form.

They all came to the capital. The king placed *Dhruva* on the throne and retired into a jungle with his two dear wives. *Dhruva* ruled for many years and made his kingdom a land of happiness and bliss.

SABITRI AND SATYAVAN.

[1]

ASWAPATI was the king of *Abani*; He was a ruler beloved of all his people. None was so good, just and generous as he.

He had a most beautiful and charming daughter, named *Sábitri*. Poets say that she was as beautiful as *Lakshmi* and as accomplished as *Saraswati*.* Her heart and mind were as grand as her external appearance. She was the gem that adorned the royal court of *Abani*.

*** *Lakshmi* is the Goddess of Wealth and supposed to be the impersonation of Beauty. *Saraswati* is the Goddess of Fine Arts and supposed to be the embodiment of all accomplishments.**

She often went out with her maid, and travelled over many parts of her father's kingdom. Once, she came to the holy-seat of *Rishis* and there she met with a young man, named *Satyaván*. She was much impressed with his beauty, grace and amiability. She talked with him and she soon fell in love with him. She despatched one of her maids to enquire who the youngman was ; she returned home leaving her heart behind which was too beautiful to be lost.

The maid came and told her that the name of the youngman was *Satyaván* ; he was the son of king *Dumetsena* of *Abanti*, who had been driven out of his kingdom and who had been living in this holy-seat as an anchorite with his wife and son some years past. *Sábitri* was very much pleased to learn that her lover was of royal parentage ; as for his present poverty it did not matter much, for she was the heir-apparent of her father's kingdom.

She went to her mother and told her that she had made a choice of a husband ; it was *Satyaván* living in the hermitage.* The queen told her royal husband what she had heard from her daughter. The king wanted to consult with his ministers and

* Readers must have marked that in ancient India there was no seclusion of women. They were not married early and they had a free hand in making choice of their husbands.

especially with the *Rishi Nárada* ;* for personally he was not willing to give away his charming daughter to an anchorite boy.

Fortunately one day *Nárada* appeared in his court and the king was spared the trouble of hunting him out,—for the great *Rishi* used to be always on the move. King *Aswapati* told him all that had happened and the resolve that his daughter had made to marry the boy of the forest. "Oh king," said *Nárada*, "Give up the idea of this marriage. You cannot marry your daughter to *Satyaván*." The king grew anxious and asked the reason. "*Satyaván*," said the *Rishi*, "is as well-born as you,—he is as well-educated as any other prince in India. Surely he is the fittest match for your beautiful and accomplished daughter, but alas, fatality,—a sad fatality,—hangs over his head. He will die just a year after from this date."

Who could possibly marry his beloved daughter to a man who is destined to die within a year? Both the king and the queen tried their utmost to induce *Sábitri* to give up the idea of this marriage,—but she was resolute. Love rose above all other considerations. She determined to marry *Satyaván*, knowing full well that she was running a great risk by doing it.

* In fact *Nárada* was a match-making *Rishi*. It is said that he was also a quarrel-breeding *Rishi*.

Her parents had to yield. Her marriage was solemnized and she left the capital and went to live with her husband in his forest-abode. The royal Princess went away to become a holy *Sanyasini.**

[2]

THERE in that miserable hut she lived the most happy life. She nursed her old and broken down father and mother-in-law ; she cooked their meals, she did all the works of that happy household. Thus a year past and at last the fatal day came. *Satyaván* knew nothing of it,—but *Sábitri* never forgot the dreadful words that fell from the great *Rishi.* She calculated the day to a minute and resolved to be by her dear husband's side at the fatal moment.

Satyaván was hastening out into the forest to collect fire-woods and fruits ; *Sábitri* glided past her father-in-law and came to his side. "My Lord," entreated she, "Allow me to accompany you to the forest." "Well," replied *Satyaván* smiling "What a whim ? Could you walk into a forest full of thorns and weeds ! I shall be back in no time." But, no,—she would have no refusal. She most entreatingly asked him to allow her to go. *Satyaván* smiled and said, "Come then ; you will never again wish to go, I am sure."

* It means a female anchorite.

They clasped each other's hands, and merrily they went and disappeared into the wilderness of the great forest. They gathered various sorts of fruits and *Sábitri's* basket grew more than full. They then plucked various sorts of wild flowers; and the wife decorated the husband and the husband the wife. Oh how happy were they! Time flew they knew not how and the sun rolled down the western horizon. "My sweet darling," said *Satyaván*, "it has already become evening,—let us hasten home. But look,—I have forgotten to collect the fire-woods altogether."

He at once got upon a tree and began to gather dried twigs. But he soon cried, "*Sábitri*, my wife dear, suddenly I have got severe head-ache. I do not know what it is;—Oh, I am dying!" "Come down," replied *Sábitri* with difficulty, "A little rest will make you all right."

He came down and lay on the grass resting his head on her lap,—but he soon became very restless;—he rose up and kissed his beloved wife and fell dead. In the deep forest, amongst all sorts of wild beasts, *Sábitri* sat with the corpse of her husband;—Night slowly and silently began to envelope the world with her sable cloth;—all was darkness.

The messengers of *Yama** came to take away the soul of the dead *Satayván*, but they found the body

* *Yama* is the Hindu Pluto.

enveloped in celestial fire. A lady was sitting on whose laps the head of the dead man rested. The fire was issuing forth from the wonderful being,—and none could dare approach her.* The messengers of Death fled in dismay and reported to their king all that they had seen in the forest.

Yama himself went to see what the matter was. He saw *Sábitri* sitting with the head of her dead husband on her lap. The terrible king of Death found it difficult to go near her. He stood aloof and addressed her. "Good and great *Sábitri*," said he, "Your husband is dead. None lives for ever in this world. Give up your husband, so that I might take him to the other world. What is the good of remaining with one who is no more?" *Sábitri* silently rose and left the corpse.

Yama instantly took the soul out of the body of the dead *Satyaván* and hastened away. But when he had gone some distance, he heard foot-steps behind; he looked back and found *Sábitri* following him.† "My good girl," said the Black King,‡ "Where are you going with me? No living man goes there." "But Oh God," said *Sábitri*, "A wife is bound to follow her

* Evidently all this means that a chaste, faithful and loving wife is a goddess whom even Pluto dares not touch.

† The latter portion of this tale appears to be allegorical.

‡ *Yama* is supposed to be very dark.

husband wherever he goes." "But," said *Yama*, "This is quite a different case. Your husband is dead and you are living; you cannot follow him. No, my good girl,—go back home. I shall grant you any thing you ask,—but allow me to go with the Life of your husband." "Oh kind God," replied she, "If you are so pleased,—grant a son to my father. who had no sons." "Yes, it is granted," cried *Yama* and hastened away.

But he soon found that *Sábitri* was following him as before. "Again are you coming?" said he, "Ask from me any thing you like, except the life of *Satyaván*, and allow me to go away." "If you are so pleaseed" said she, "Grant sight to my father-in-law who is blind." "Granted" cried *Yama* and walked hastily away.

But still *Sábitri* was at his back. The king of darkness became really bewildered and confused. "My good girl," said he, "You cannot follow your husband any further. I entreat you to allow me to go. Ask from me any thing you like except the life of your husband." "If you so please," replied she, "Grant my father-in-law his lost kingdom." "Go home,—it is granted," said *Yama* and he began to run to get rid of the tenacious girl that was following him like a shadow. But *Sábitri* ran too;—she soon came up to him and followed him as a shadow follows a man.

The king was really bewildered. "I am ready to give you," said he "Whatever you ask,—but allow me to go to my own city. Ask anything you like except your husband's life." "If you so please," replied she, "Grant me one hundred sons from *Satyaván*." "Granted," bawled out the king and ran. But *Sabitri* was still at his back. *Yama* at last halted, turned back and addressed *Sábitri* thus, "My dear girl, you are trying to do what is impossible. I say, your husband is dead and there is not the least chance of your getting him back or following him where he is going." "Oh great God," replied she, "I have no mind to go with you;—but you have granted my prayer that I shall get one hundred sons from *Satyaván*. I know your words would never be false;—but I do not understand how I shall get sons from *Satyaván* whom you are taking away with you."

The king of darkness stared in dismay; but he was much pleased with the intelligence and fidelity of *Sábitri*. "Most excellent girl," said he, "You are really a goddess. Your love and faith towards your husband is more than exemplary. As a reward to your great character, I shall for once do an act which was never done before. Go back,—your husband is saved."

* * * *

Sábitri hastened back to the forest; she took up the head of her husband and placed it on her lap.

Satyaván soon opened his eyes and saw darkness all around. "*Sábitri,*" said he, "How is it that I fell asleep ? Is it night ?" "Yes," replied she, "You were tired and I did not think it proper to disturb you."

They soon started for home, where their parents were very much anxious for them. What was their joy when they saw their son with his wife safe at home !

We need not mention that all that was granted by king *Yama* was duly received. King *Aswapati* got a son, the old king of *Abanti* got back his sight and his lost kingdom, and *Sabitri* her one hundred sons.

DEBJANI.

[1]

THE great *Rishi Sukra* was the Preceptor of the *Dánavas.* He had a most charming daughter, named *Debjáni.* She was as fair as the fairest of the fairies; as learned as her great father and as accomplished as the beautiful Goddess of Learning. She lived in the forest-home of her father as a lily, blossomed in the wilderness of Nature; she cast a halo of joy wherever she went.

She loved *Kacha*, one of her father's pupils; but he did not love her in the way she did. He had the highest admiration, the greatest respect and a brother's affection for her,—but nothing more. Now *Kacha* was the son of *Brihaspati*, the great Preceptor of the gods. He was sent in disguise to learn from the Preceptor of the *Dánavas* what he had to teach and what he taught the demons. He went and became a pupil of great *Sukra* and learnt from him all that he had to teach. Thus years passed on, till the *Dánavas* came to learn that the boy was no other than the son of *Brihaspati*. They at once resolved to murder him.

When one day *Kacha* went to the pasture with his tutor's cows, the *Dánavas* set upon him and killed him. Night drew on,—and *Kacha* did not return home. One by one all the cows came back to the *Asrama*,*—but there was no *Kacha* with them. *Debjáni* grew very much anxious for him,—more than ten thousand times, she eagerly went out of her father's cottage to see if *Kacha* was returning; but night rolled on,—soon it became mid-night,—still *Kacha* did not return home. She went to her father and burst into tears. "My dear girl," asked the *Rishi*, "Has any body offended you? Why are you weeping?" She told him what had happened. "Well," said *Sukra*, "You need not be anxious for him. If he is dead, still I can give him life again." He immersed himself for a while in *Yoga* and then

* An *Asrama* means the holy seat of a *Rishi*.

called out thrice the name of *Kacha*; instantly the boy appeared at the gate of the *Asrama*.

The *Dánavas* were disappointed; they dared not openly kill *Kacha*, for they knew he was the most favourite pupil of the great *Rishi*. They knew also that *Debjáni* madly loved the boy, and the old *Rishi's* love for his daughter, knew no bounds. They resolved to murder the boy secretely and to do something which would prevent the *Rishi* from giving him life again. When *Kacha* went out to gather flowers for *Debjáni*, he was again set upon by the *Dánavas* and killed. They dressed his flesh and cooked it; they invited the Preceptor to the feast and gave him drink. The *Rishi*, being drunk and not knowing what he was eating, made the best possible dinner on the flesh of his most favourite pupil.

Kacha did not return home; *Debjáni* went to her father when he returned from the demon-feast and told him that *Kacha* had not come back. "Father," said she sobbing, "The wicked *Dánavas* must have again killed him. If you do not bring him back, I shall kill myself,—for without *Kacha* I cannot live."

The great *Rishi* was horrified to learn through his *Yoga*-insight* that he himself had eaten up his

* Read a brief account of *Yoga* in the Appendix.

favourite boy.* However, he gave life to *Kacha* in his stomach and taught him the great *Mantra*† of reviving life. "*Kacha*," said the *Rishi*, "I have taught you the great secret; I shall now render open my stomach. Come out and give me life by the help of the *Mantra*." So it was done. *Kacha* came out of his tutor's stomach and gave life to him by uttering the *Mantra*.

Kacha thought that it was high time for him to return to heaven. He got permission from his Preceptor to go and went to *Debjáni* to bid her farewell. She would not allow him to go. She offered her hand to him, she gave vent to all her pent up feelings, she expressed the great love that she bore for him. "*Debjáni*," said *Kacha*, "You are the daughter of my Preceptor and therefore you are a sister to me. I cannot marry you. You are a sensible and learned girl,‡ you must excuse me."

* It is said that after this sad occurrence *Sukra* issued an edict prohibiting drinking and calling it a great sin. Since then drinking has become a religious sin and a moral vice in India.

† *Mantras* are some peculiar letters and words *uttered*, in a peculiar way. It is said there are various sorts of *Mantras* to produce various wonderful and miraculous results.

‡ Readers must have marked that the women of ancient India used to get education of a very high order. *Khaná* and *Lilábati* were great mathemeticians and astronomers. When *Sankaráchárya*, the greatest of the Hindu Reformers went to the great

Debjáni took offence. When a woman's pride and vanity are wounded, she becomes furious as ten furies; she cursed her lover and left him in great rage.

[2]

Brishaparba was the name of the *Dánava* king who ruled over the demon-sovereignty when great *Sukra* was stopping in their kingdom. The king had a most beautiful daughter, named *Sharmisthá* ;* She was beautiful, but proud; accomplished, but way-ward; but she was very dutiful and religious. *Debjáni* and *Sharmisthá* were friends ;—outwardly they expressed the greatest friendship for each

Philosopher *Manduk Missra* to defeat him in Philosophy, he found it easy to defeat him,—but not his wife. She was so learned that *Shankaráchárya* took six month's time to prepare himself to debate with her.

* We think we should mention here that in this tale the readers will find some difference in the demon-character from that which they have found in the first tale in this Book. Originally the bad *Elements* were allegorically called the *Dánavas*, or the demons ; but it is evident that the later writers forgot its original use and began to use it with regard to aboriginal tribes, *i. e.* non-aryan people, whom they christened as *Dánavas*. It would be apparent from this tale that king *Brishaparba* and Princess *Sharmisthá* are not allegorical characters, but a king and a princess of the non aryan tribe.

other; but inwardly they never agreed. *Debjáni* was jealous of *Sharmistha* for her wealth and position. The Princess was jealous of the ascetic's daughter for her great learning and high social honour. However, they were too sensible to quarrel and passed the time in amity and friendship.

Once they all went to bathe in a beautiful lake. *Sharmistha* went with her innumerable maids and she invited her Preceptor's daughter to accompany her. They all went and amused themselves in the crystal water of the beautiful *Sarobara.** But they were disturbed in their merry pastime;†—they hastened to the bank where they left their clothes and hurriedly dressed themselves. In the confusion that followed, the Princess put on the cloth of *Debjáni,* for which she took terrible offence. *Sharmistha* was a *Sudra* and *Debjáni* was a *Brahmin*;‡ a lady of her caste could reasonably take offence for the act done by the *Dánava* princess. "Oh proud and arrogant girl,"

---

* *Sarobara* means a beautiful lake.

† It is said that the cause of the ladies' hastening towards their clothes was the approach of *Shiva*, who was passing by the lake.

‡ We believe readers are aware that the Hindus are divided into four principal castes, namely, *Brahmin*, *Kshatriya*, *Baishya* and *Sudra*. The last is the servant caste and was originally recruited from the non-aryan tribes. We need not say that they were the most hated, specially by the *Brahmins*.

cried *Debjáni*, "How dare you wear my cloth ? Do you not know whose daughter I am." The Princess retorted and there was a great quarrel between the two. At last the Princess with the help of her maids threw *Debjáni* into an well and there they left her to die a most painful death.

But *Debjáni* was not to die then. The great king *Yayáti** came to hunt and went to the well for water, in which poor *Debjáni* was lying. He saw her and immediately tried to lift her up from her painful situation. She caught hold of his out-streached hand and came out of the well. "My Lord," said she, "You have accepted my hands,—you have therefore become my husband. I cannot take any other husband." The king was much pleased with her exquisite beauty and great learning ; he agreed to marry her, and married her then and there in the *Gandharva* way. "My sweet darling," said the king, "As soon as I shall return to my capital, I shall send men to fetch you."

Debjáni returned home and told her father all that had happened and all that wicked and proud *Sharmistha* had done. She wept and would not be consoled. When her fond father pressed her very much to say what she wanted, she sobbed and said, "Father, nothing but *Sharmistha's* becoming my

* He was a king of the Lunar Dynasty.

maid-servant, would satisfy me for the gross insult she had done me."

The Preceptor of the *Dânavas* called for the king. He told him in great anger what his daughter had done. He threatened to curse the king with all his people and then to leave the kingdom for good. *Brishaparba* apologised for the misconduct of his daughter ; he fell on his knees and entreated him to pardon him. He humbly prayed to be inflicted with any punishment except his leaving him and his kingdom. "King," said the *Rishi*, "Give me your daughter ; I shall make her my *Debjáni's* maid." "I shall make her do it," said the king and hastened to the palace to bring her to the *Rishi's* cottage.

When the king told his daughter what the great *Rishi* wanted of her, she gently said, "Father, for you and for the sake of my race, I shall glady become the maid-servant of *Debjáni*. I know she wants to satisfy her old grudge,—let her do it. I am prepared to suffer every indignity for the good of my parents." She went to the *Rishi's* cottage and thenceforth remained as the obedient and humble servant of the daughter of great *Sukra*.

A few days after, king *Yayáti* sent his men to the *Rishi's Asrama* to take away his bride. *Debjáni* left her forest-home for the royal palace at *Hastinápura*, and *Sharmisthá* accompanied her.

[3]

Both king *Yayáti* and princess *Sharmisthá* when they met, fell in love with each other ; but the king was afraid of his wife ; *Debjáni* ruled him with an iron hand. However, they secretely met and passed their time most happily for years, till three sons were born to *Sharmisthá*. *Debjáni* gave birth to two princes and they all lived happily for many years.

One day *Debjáni* went to see her maid *Sharmisthá* in her own quarters ; she saw the youngest of her sons, who was named *Puru* playing with some boys. *Debjáni* never knew that *Sharmisthá* had a son,—how could she get a son when she had no husband ? But she was struck with the appearance of the boy ; she went to him and asked him the name of his father. "My father !" said the child, "You know him not ! He is king *Yayáti*." *Debjáni's* countenance flashed fire, but she suppressed her indignant feelings and said, "My sweet child, who is the happy woman whom you call your mother ?" "Why," cried the child, "Queen *Sharmisthá* is my mother !" We need not say, *Debjáni's* anger knew no bounds ; she at once left the palace and went weeping to her great father. Soon the news reached the king; he hastened in pursuit of her, so that he might appease her great anger. He was terribly afraid of the great *Sukra* and his curses; he was perfectly aware that as soon as the great *Rishi* would hear the complaints of his daughter he would be sure to shower upon him the bitterest curses.

As he apprehended, when the great *Rishi* heard from his weeping daughter that the king had behaved most faithlessly and had neglected her—his eyes rolled and his hairs stood upon their end out of anger. "You have become faithless to my daughter," said the *Rishi* "on account of the cravings of your youth of which you perhaps take pride. Let dotage of the old age overtake you and teach you there is nothing to be proud of."*

What could be severer punishment than this? Is it not more than death to one who is in his prime of life to suddenly find himself in old age? The king fell cn his knees and prayed for mercy; he most humbly craved for pardon; he expressed his great regret and repented for what he had done. *Debjáni* was moved to see the humiliation of her husband; she felt the greatest possible pain when she saw his beautiful figure and graceful

* Even now the Hindus are terribly afraid of the curses of Brahmins. Perhaps in times gone by the *Rishis* by their *Yoga* faculties could *defacto* perform what they said.

youth turn into the decrepit old age. Really she loved him,—she repented for her rashness and entreated her father to save her dear husband. "My dear daughter," said the *Rishi*, "It is now too late. However, if any of his children wilfully take upon himself the old age that has overtaken him, he can get back his youth and enjoy it as long as he wishes."

The king returned to his capital, and called his five sons to him,—two of *Debjáni* and three of *Sharmisthá*. He asked them one after another,—if any of them was willing to take upon himself the old age that had suddenly overtaken him. Each and every one of them refused to suffer for their father, except *Puru*, the youngest son of *Sharsmisthá*. "Father," said he, "I am bound to obey you. I have got my life from you and what is more glorious than to give that life for your benefit. Give me your old age and I shall be very happy to see you again as you were before."

So it was done. *Puru* became a decrepit old man in his worst dotage and the king enjoyed his youth in luxury and pleasure.

But soon *Yajáti* repented for his love of pleasure. It pained him to see his dear son suffer the worst possible pains for his cupidity. He took back the old age from *Puru* ; he placed him on the throne as his successor and then he finally retired into the forest with his two wives to meditate and to pray.

BILWAMANGALA.

[1]

THERE was in ancient time a very rich young-man, whose name was *Bilwamangala.* He was brought up in luxury and afluence, in flattery and indulgence. He. was surrounded by low companions and bad women ;—his life was a continual stream of debauchery and carnality.

At last he fell in love with a woman, named *Chintámani*. She was beautiful, accomplished and young ; she was intelligent, clever and sharp ; she understood human nature thoroughly well and knew how to mould and control it. She gradually spread a wonderful influence over the youngman and ruled him with an iron hand. He lost himself in her magic enticements ; he forgot himself with her satanic wiles ; he put himself in her hand to be played like a doll.

Money went away like water ; costly things and valuable jewellery were heaped at her feet ;—finally *Bilwamangala* left his home and remained day and night with her. Again and again his old father sent men to bring him home,—his poor mother wept and wept, till she became almost blind ; his friends entreated and his relatives prayed,—but all in vain. He did not and could not leave the Syren's house where some unknowable infatuation kept him chained.

At last his old father died, and died of a broken-heart for the misconduct of his wild son. Men were sent to bring *Bilwamangala* home to perform his father's last rites,—but he did not come. Without him the *Sráddha* ceremony* could not be performed ;—so his relatives went to *Chintámani* and appealed to her to allow him to go at least for a day to save the spirit of the dead man from the eternal hell-fire. *Chintámani* was moved ; she pressed him to go ; and when he refused to go, she positively drove him out of her house.

* It is a ceremony performed on the 10th day after death for Brahmins and a month after for other castes in honour of the departed spirit. It is further said that unless this *Sráddha* ceremony is performed by the son, the soul of the parents cannot leave this world and go to heaven.

Being forced to leave her for a few hours, he went home with a sorrowful heart. As quick as possible he went through the ceremony ;—every second moment he tried to slip out and fly to *Chintámani's* house. But notwithstanding all efforts he could not leave his house before evening. When he left his house and hastened towards his lady-love ; it was already night.

[2]

It was a dreadful night ; the sky was full of black clouds,—lightning was flashing from one corner of the horizon to the other,—fearful thunder was roaring, shaking the earth to its very centre ; rain was falling like torents,—a great and tremendous storm had burst all over the earth. Trees were uprooted and houses were shattered ;—birds were crushed into atoms and beasts were killed in hundreds. No living creature was safe in the furious storm that was raging outside. Mad *Bilwamangala* rushed out of his house to hasten to his love and was knocked about in the storm, as he ran towards the river side, across which lay the house of *Chintámani*. He was mad ; he forgot in the fervor of love that he bore for the woman that the elements were engaged in a mortal fight. More than hundred times he lost his footing by the force of the wind and got severe bruises all over the body. But nothing could prevent him from proceeding ; he came at last to the river, which was roaring and foaming in a mad fury.

How to cross it ? He saw something floating in the river, he thought it to be a peice of wood and jumped into the river to catch hold of it. He was successful,—he floated resting on it and was carried away by the strong current, where he knew not. However, luck was not against him,—somehow or other he reached the opposite shore and ran towards the house of the woman who had made him mad.

Her house was surrounded by a high wall ; her door was locked from inside,—he again and again called her out,—but his voice was drowned in the tremendous roars of the furious storm. He then tried to scale the wall,—and ran round and round the house to find out, if there were any means to do it. At last he saw something hanging from the wall ;—Oh, he was so happy,—he thought it to be a piece of rope and immediately caught hold of it. He dragged himself by its help up on the top of the wall ; then he jumped down into the yard and rushed into the house.

[3]

CHINTAMANI was astonished to find *Bilwamangala* at that dreadful hour. How could he manage to come! How could he venture out in the great storm that was fearfully raising outside? What a nausiating stink that was coming out of him! "Beloved *Chintámani*," said the youngman, "I have come." "Who told you to come," replied she, "Who told you to risk your life in this fearful storm?" "Oh *Chintámani*," exclaimed he, "You do not know how much I love you." "But how could you manage to cross the river," asked she, "And scale the wall?" *Bilwamangala* told her what he had done and how he had been able to come to her.

By the time the storm much abated; *Chintámani* knew that there was no rope any where hanging from her wall; she was very much curious to learn how he had managed to scale it. She came out with a light and accompanied by *Bilwamangala* she went to that portion of the wall where he said the rope was hanging. But what was her horror when she found the said rope to be nothing else but a most deadly snake! She wildly stared at the youngman and could not utter a word. Then she ran towards the river which passed by just below her house to see what other horrible thing he got hold of to cross the river. Oh horror of horrors! it was not a piece of wood; it was a dead body, a rotten and putrid corpse which the mad young man caught hold of to cross the furious river. When she saw it, she burst into tears. "*Bilwamangala*," exclaimed she, "I now know that you really love me, but I am not worthy of your great love. Oh, how good it would have been if you had dedicated your this unknowable love to God!"

The word went into the very depth of the youngman's heart; he stood a few seconds in mute astonishment; then he said, "Yes, *Chintámani*, you are right."

He immedcately left the place, and though she ran after him and tried to prevent him from going, yet he went away and never returned to see her, for whom he was once mad.

He went away and became a hermit;—years rolled on and *Bilwamangala* became one of the greatest devotees.*

* There is another tale which is almost akin to it, though the incidents were not the same. A leper Brahmin once saw a most charming woman for whom he grew mad. His most loving wife finding him melancholy pressed him to tell her the cause of his misery. At last he told her that he would commit suicide if he did not get her. The loving wife went to the woman and became her maid-servant to make her husband happy. Soon

she made her so much pleased with her that she asked her what favour she wanted from her. "Oh Lady," said she, "If you are so very kind, allow my husband to come to you one day." She heard from the poor wife all that had happened and agreed to allow him to come. He prepared for him a best dinner and placed two glasses by his side, one full of crystal water and other with mudy Ganges water. The leper Bramhin at the time of drinking, drank from the glass, in which there was the water of the holy Ganges. "Why Sir," asked the woman, "You drink that mudy water instead of the crystal water that is in the other glass?" "Well," replied the poor Bramhin. "You see, it is the water of the holy Ganges,"—"Why then Sir,' said she, "You neglect the holy water at home and come to drink crystal water here?" She meant by the holy water his wife and by the crystal water herself. Her words went deep into the man's heart; he at once rose and left her house and thenceforth became a most loving husband.

HARISHCHANDRA.

[1]

KING *Harishchandra* was one of the most celebrated rulers of the Solar Dynasty. He was as powerful as mighty, as virtuous as good; none there was so charitable and such a supporter of learning and religion as he. But with all his goodness and love of religion he incurred the anger of one of the most powerful and terrible *Rishis*.

Viswámitra was a great *Rishi*; he was originally not a Brahmin. Perhaps we need not say that in those ancient days Brahmins only were allowed to study religion and philosophy,—they only were permitted to be *Rishis* and *ascetics*, but *Viswámitra* broke through the rule ; he studied *Vedas* and practised *Yoga* and finally raised himself up to a position higher than all the *Rishis* of the period. He was as high-spirited and hot tempered as he was learned ; he was as mighty as he was religious ; people were afraid of him ; the great chiefs and potentates feared his frowns.

He lived in a great forest,—far far away from all habitations, but his hermitage was a very beautiful place, surrounded by charming gardens and enchanting groves. Fragrant flowers smiled at every step and many-coloured creepers playfully entwined his simple hut. He lived in solitude and in his own meditations, adoring the gods with flowers that blossomed round his cottage.

His holy-seat was so charming that some fairies took pleasure to come to his gardens and play there with his beautiful flowers. Whenever the great *Rishi* went in the morning to gather flowers to worship his gods, he found that merciless havock had been made in his garden over his most favourite flowers. He knew not who could dare pluck his flowers and destroy the beauty of his garden. Every day he wondered and every day he found that some body had come to his garden and topsy-turvied it in every possible way. To find out the mischief-makers he so arranged that next time, whoever they might be, if they at all would come, they would be caught in the net of creepers that were all around the garden.

The fairies as usual came at the dead of night and went to play in their old haunts. They were immediately caught in the net and although they struggled much, they could not get out of the mess of creepers. Oh, how piteously they looked at each other,—how they exerted all their strength to break assunder the dreadful creepers,—how much they wished to get out of the fearful garden and to be far away from its most fearful master,—but all their efforts were in vain. When they found they had been imprisoned and there was no hope of escape, they all burst into tears. Alas, they were but women ; they were terribly afraid of incurring the anger of *Rishi Viswámitra*.

Their lamentations and piteous cry reached the ear of king *Harishchandra*, who came out for hunting. Fearing that some mishap had fallen on some helpless women, he hastened to their help. He found that some fairies had been imprisoned in the net of creepers,—he never paused to think of the cause of their imprisonment, his galantry rose over all his feelings,—he immediately took out his weapon and liberated them all. They thanked him from the depth of their heart and fled to their mountain-homes, resolving never to set foot again in the garden of the fearful *Rishi*. King *Harischandra*, never dreaming that this small incident would be the cause of his future ruin and misery, returned to his capital after his hunting excursion all over the forest.

[2]

THE great *Rishi Viswámitra* went in the morning to see who had been caught in the net set by him, but to his great disappointment and displeasure he found that some body had cut assunder all his creepers and set free those that were caught in the net. The great *Rishi's* anger knew no bounds,—fire flashed from his eyes. "Who is the arrogant man," exclaimed he, "that dares interfere with the works of *Viswámitra*."

He soon found that the great king *Harishchandra* came to his holy seat and set free the fairies whom he had a mind to punish for their impudent interference with his garden. "Well," said the *Rishi*, "It seems that the man has become very arrogant and proud of his wealth and high position. He will soon learn what it is to offend *Viswámitra*." He resolved upon taking vengeance,—he determined to teach the proud king a severe lesson who had unwittingly incurred his displeasure.

He left his holy seat and appeared in the court of the great king. He was received with all the honour due to his exalted position; the king remained standing before the *Rishi* and asked him with folded hands what he could do to serve the great man. "Well, king *Harishchandra*," said the *Rishi*, "You want to serve me! They say you are a very religious man and have the highest respect for us. But will you be able to satisfy *me*?" "Great and reverend Sir," replied the king, "My life, my wealth, my possessions, I consider all this nothing before the pleasure of men like you." "Well," said *Viswámitra*, "Promise me then that whatever I shall ask, you will at once grant me." The king folded his hands and most humbly said, "I promise, Oh Sir, to grant you whatever you would want." The *Rishi* smiled and then turning round to the assembly said, "Gentlemen, you have heard the promise solemnly made by this king." Then he faced the king and said, "Give me your kingdom with all that you possess."

The assembled people stared at one another,—ministers became grave and the commanders shook their arms,—for the king was the most beloved of all. But king *Harishchandra* left his throne and came near the *Rishi*; he again folded his hands and said, "Oh great *Rishi*, my people are happy to get you as their king and ruler. From to-day this kingdom is yours with all its regalia;—every thing that is in the palace, every thing that I possess,—henceforth all belongs to you. Bless me, I retire into the jungle." "Yes," said the great *Rishi*, "I praise your nobleness,—I admire your charitable feelings. You can go."

King *Harishchandra* with his good wife *Saibyá* and their son *Rohitáshwa* left the palace and went to live far away from their capital; they went to the holy pilgrimage of Benares and there they lived as best they could in their self-imposed poverty. But the heartless *Rishi* was not satisfied by making the good king a poor man. He soon followed him and appeared before him. "*Harishchandra*," said he, "I forgot to tell you when you so nobly gave me your kingdom, that no *Dána** is acceptable without the *Dakshiná*.† Where is my *Dakshiná*? Give it to me." Poor *Harishchandra* knew not what to do; he had nothing to give to the great *Rishi*. He asked a week's time to procure the required sum and to pay it to him. "Well," said *Viswámitra*, "I allow you the time, but take care to pay me on the promised day."

* *Dána* means things bestowed upon a Brahmin.

† *Dakshiná* means the coin, (*i. e.* something cash besides the things bestowed), which one is bound to give when he bestows any thing on a Brahmin.

[3]

A WEEK was a very short time to procure the required sum; the last day came, but still no money had been procured. "*Saibyá*," exclaimed the king, "We became poor to earn virtue, but alas, luck is against us! To bestow things upon a *Rishi* asked by him is a great virtue indeed,—but without the *Dakshiná* the bestower secures nothing. So all that we did was done for nothing." "My Lord," replied the good queen, "I still belong to you. Sell me to some one and get money to pay the *Dakshiná*." Oh, it was the cruelest cut of all! The king turned away his face and supressed the tears that were rushing into his eyes.

But the terrible *Rishi* was at their door; he had no mercy, no heart, no feeling. "Where is my *Dakshiná*?" cried he, "Come, look sharp, I cannot wait." Well, he might curse, he might do a thousand other mischiefs. The king grew desperate,—he came out with his wife and child; he prayed for half an hour's time. "Oh great *Rishi*," said he, "I am sorry to say that I have not been able to procure the sum. However, kindly wait half an hour. I have determined to sell my dear wife and get the money for you." "Very well," replied the cruel *Rishi*, "I shall wait."

King *Harishchandra* took his wife to the market-place and the great queen of a Royal house was placed before the public gaze. He again and again called out for a customer, but none appeared to purchase the poor queen. At last an old Brahmin came to him and wanted to inspect the woman whom he had put to sale. The king pointed out to him his most beloved wife, whom the man began to stare and to cut yokes at in an outrageous manner. The king with a super-human effort controlled his temper and settled the price with him. We need not attempt to describe the feelings of poor *Saibyá,*—well, she was a woman with unmatched patience and fortitude, or else who could stand the sufferings that she had to undergo?

"My dear husband," sobbed the queen, "Take away my *Rohitáshwa,*—he is mere a child. From to-day you become his mother and father both." "Well," said the old Brahmin, "I never knew that a man when he purchases a cow, does not purchase the calf with it. I have purchased the woman by paying ready-money. I am not going to be cheated out of the boy." He ordered the poor queen to follow him with her son and then majestically walked away from the market-place.

The sale of the queen did not fetch much money; it was far below the amount that would be required to be given to the great *Rishi.* How to raise the balance of the money ! The king determined to sell himself ; he was ready to be made an ever-lasting slave provided the money for the *Dakshiná* was forthcoming. He again and again offered himself for sale,—but there was no customer. At last a *Chandála,* who was in charge of the burning *ghát** came to him and agreed to purchase him. "Yes," said he, "I require a man for helping me in burning dead bodies. You look hale and hearty and may suit me well." A price was soon settled, and the king was paid the money. He went with it to the great *Rishi* and told him that he had brought the sum for the *Dakshiná.* "Well said *Viswámitra,* "I am now well-satisfied." He then left the king to his fate and went away. The king accompanied the *Chandála* and became the help-mate of the man who was the custodian of the place, where the last remains of men, women and children were burnt to ashes.

* It means the place where the dead bodies are burnt. These places are always in the charge of *Chandálas,* which is the most degraded and hated caste amongst the Hindus. These men help the friends of the deacesed to burn the body for a small consideration.

[4]

THE old Brahmin, who purchased the poor queen, was a miserly demon and a heartless ruffian. He was a man without any feelings for any man or woman of the world. He loved money and money was the god of his adoration. He purchased the poor queen by paying money; he, therefore, forced her to labour like a beast of burden and treated her most cruelly. Her life at his house was an unbroken chain of misery and persecution. But *Saibyá* suffered all in silence. She starved herself in order to feed her most beloved *Rohitáshwa*. She had lost her dear husband, she had lost her kingdom, she had lost all her earthly comforts, she had become the slave of a very cruel and heartless man, but there was her lovely *Rohitáshwa* by her side to comfort and console her; he was the only light in her life of misery and pain.

But alas, Misery had taken her for her own! One day when the boy went out to play with his mates, a deadly snake bit him; he came crying home and soon became pale, for the deadly poison spread all over his body. Oh, how the poor mother cried with her dying son on her lap,—how she prayed for help; how she piteously wept,—but alas, none came to her rescue! None pitied her and none said a word of sympathy for her great affliction. But the cruel Brahmin upbraided her for her loud lamentations and drove her out of his house.

Rohitáshwa breathed his last on the lap of his weeping mother; it was night,—very dark and very tempestuous; not a human being could stir out,—Nature was in her furious mood. The corpse that lay on her lap, was to be burnt;—the sweet thing that was the joy and object of love and caress, was to be placed on the funeral pyre to be burnt to ashes; no amount of weepings and lamentations would help her! She took up the boy and went weeping to the burning *Ghát*.

But, alas, even the poorest of the poor requires money to burn or bury the last remains of those that once were dear and near to them. The thought never occurred to her; in her great bereavement she forgot that she would require money to destroy the last semblance of her dearest boy. She came to the *Ghát*, it was dreary and dark; a solitary *Chandál* was sitting on the bank of the river, immersed in his own thoughts. Even the most degraded of the human beings had his thoughts to dwell upon! He rose up when he heard wailings behind him. Pity and sorrow no longer arose in his breast for the sad and most painful bereavements of others; so many men, women and children he had burnt,—so many bereaved parents, relatives and friends he had seen, that no longer any emotion stirred into his mind. He came near *Saibyâ* and damanded the usual fee. Alas, where would she get it,—she had not a pice to spare! When the money was demanded, she wept the more.

When the *Chandál* came with his light to see the dead body,—it fell on the face of the bereaved mother. The recognition was instantaneous. *Saibyá* fell on the breast of her husband and sobbed out, "Oh, look at my *Rohitáshwa*; he is no more." We need not describe the scene,—it was heart-rending.

When the bereaved parents, when the most unfortunate king and his most unhappy queen, were bewailing over the corpse of their most beloved son, *Rishi Viswámitra* appeared on the scene. "King," said he, "You grew very proud and arrogant, and that is the reason why I made you come so low and why you have suffered unbearable woes. But you have come out of the trial victorious. You have by your most noble deed secured a name which will give lusture to generations to come. Bring the child to me,—I shall revive it. Go back to your kingdom,—it is yours."

The *Rishi* gave life to the corpse of the dead prince. Next day the king and the queen with their son started for their capital. There was joy and merriment all over the kingdom; and they were very very happy.

King *Harishchandra* and queen *Saibyá* lived for many years. None there was in their kingdom who had any wants. Poor men had only to come at the Royal palace and point out their grievances; religious men had only to send words to his court and all their demands were supplied. Happy were the people that lived under the benign rule of king *Harishchandra*.

PARASURAMA.

[1]

A GREAT hero rose from the rank c Brahmins and thrice seven times he defeated and conquered the *Kshatryas*, who were the most powerful warrior-caste of the ancient Hindus. This hero was *Parasuráma*, the son of *Jámadagni*, one of the most celebrated *Rishis* of ancient India. Away from the noisy world the old *Rishi* lived in the solitude of a great forest, adoring the unknowable ONE and meditating upon His wonderful Creation. Thus years after years rolled away in studying the *Vedas** and practising the *Yoga*. At last the *Rishi*

* The *Vedas* are the most holy and ancient books of the Hindus, and are considered to be the words of God. *Rik*, *Yayu*,

came out of his solitary abode and travelled all over the country, till he came to the kingdom of Raja *Prasanajit*. The king had a most charming daughter, named *Renuká*, whom the *Rishi* saw and thought of marrying. The mighty Ruler dared not refuse him ; he gave away his daughter to the ascetic Brahmin, who took her away to his forest-home.

Princess *Renuká* was virtuous and good ; she was a most faithful wife and a dutiful help-mate ot her husband. She never complained for the greaf change that came upon her life ; she was never sorry to live the life of an ascetic, though she was a great princess. She lived happily for years till one after another five sons were born to her, the last being the hero of this tale.

Once on a time princess *Renuká* went to bathe in the river that flowed by the side of their hermitage. She met on her way prince *Chittraratha* of *Mirtikábati* ; and alas, human heart is so weak, so frail, so unknowable, that she, who had renounced all pleasures and luxuries of a royal palace for the rigid asceticism of the forest through her strong sense of duty, fidelity and chastity, allowed unworthy thoughts to arise into her mind ! She came back disturbed to the hermitage and her husband perceived her

Sákm and *Athurba*, these are the four *Vedas*. But the *Vedas* often mean the whole of Hindu Theology.

agitations. Seeing that she had fallen from perfection and lost the lusture of sanctity, *Jámadagni* reproved her and was exceedingly angry.

There came her sons from the wood, and each, as he entered the cottage, was commanded by his father to put his mother to death. Amazed they stood silent,—how could they commit such an unnatural and horrible crime?

At last came *Parasuráma*. "Son," said the angry *Rishi*, "Kill thy mother; she has sinned." "Father," replied the son, "I must obey your command." He took up his axe and beheaded *Renuká*. "Well," said *Jámadagni*, "You have obeyed my command and done an act hard to perform. I am pleased with you and willing to grant you whatever blessings you demand." "Father," said *Parasuráma*, "If you so please, restore my mother to life and advice me what to do to expatiate the great crime and sin that I have committed by killing my mother." "Son," replied he, "I restore your mother to life and advise you to visit all the holy places to expatiate the sin that you have committed under my command."

Parasuráma left the hermitage of his father and went away to travel over the country. Here in his absence the mighty king *Kirtaviryya* came to his father's holy-seat and was received in great honour. But the proud king, instead of requiting the hospitality of the *Rishi*, took away by force the calf of the milch-cow of the holy hermitage.

When *Parsuráma* returned, he was told what had happened. He was a man of high spirit,—he was a giant in physical strength and a great warrior in arms; he at once took up his axe and went to kill the king for his most impudent conduct. There was a great fight between the two, but at last the king fell. *Parasuráma* struck off his head and took it to his father.

The sons of *Kirtaviryya* determined to revenge their father's death. They came with a large army and surrounded the holy hermitage of the old *Rishi*. Unfortunately *Parasuráma* was absent from home; thus they unopposed destroyed the holy-seat of the *Rishi*, killed him whom they could lay hand upon and slew the pious and unresisting sage. When *Parasuráma* returned home he found his father cruelly murdered and his hermitage mercilessly destroyed.

He silently performed the last obsequies of his father and placed his body on the funeral pile. When the fire blazed in great fury over the dead body of the old *Rishi*, *Parasuráma* in the name of all that was holy made a vow facing the fire that he would kill all the sons of *Kirtaviryya*,—nay he would exterminate the whole of the *Kshatriya* race from the face of the earth to revenge his father's foul murder.

With the terrible axe on his shoulder and his fearful bow and deadly arrows on his back he left his father's hermitage and came out of the forest. It was a fearful carnage he began ; he killed all the sons of *Kirtaviryya*,—nay each and every one of his royal house. He then left the place and went to kill other *Kshatriyas*. Thrice seven times he exterminated the *Kshatriya* race from the face of the earth, and filled up with *Kshatriya* blood seven big tanks. There on the banks of these bloody tanks he performed his father's *Sráddha* ceremoney and his last obsequies.

He then went to king *Janaka* and left with him his fearful bow.* Thence he retired to the holy mountains and passed his time in meditations and prayers.

* See Rámayana.

BISHAYA.

[1]

BISHAYA was a most beautiful and accomplished Princess of the Lunar Dynasty. She was the only daughter of her father and consequently the heir-apparent to the throne of his kingdom. She was the joy of her parents and beloved of all their people. She was intelligent and learned ;—she had received the education befitting her great rank and the high and responsible duties which sooner or later she would be called upon to perform.

But education, learning or accomplishments have no hold on one's heart. Sense of duty, intelligence, prudence or all the higher faculties of mind cannot control the unknowable emotion which is known by the name of love. It blossoms up in one's mind so suddenly as to take him by surprise ; it ignites as quick as gun-powder and blazes up in great fury. It never pauses to think who and what is the object of its love ; it loves and madly continues to love without knowing why it does. Princess *Bishayá* fell in love with a young man of his father's court, named *Chandrahásha.* He was an orphan boy, brought up in charity but he was handsome, educated and accomplished. He was greatly loved by the king and he was a favourite of all the court. Wherever the king went, *Chandrahásha* was sure to be by his side. The king loved him and he loved the king.

He saw the princess more than once ; he had the honour of talking with her and the pleasure of accompanying her to many places ; but he had no particular love for her. He had the highest admiration and the greatest respect for her, but not that unexplainable love which a young man feels for a young woman. He never knew,—and the thought never occurred to him,—that the princess had any other feelings for her than the ordinary sympathy and affection for one whom her father loved. He never knew that he had occupied her heart and become the sole object of her adoration.

Although no body knew it, the companions and maids of the princess knew the state of the feelings ot their mistress. She did never hid it,—she never tried to put a veil over her loving heart,—she openly and often told them that if she would marry at all, she would marry *Chandrahásha.* The maids thought it their duty to acquaint the queen with the state of her daughter's feelings ;—for the matter was a very serious one ;—she being the heir-apparent could by no means marry the unknown young man. The queen told the king what had happened. "Well," said he, "It is a serious matter no doubt. She cannot by any means marry this young man. She is sensible and educated,—convince her of her folly and induce her to give up the idea." "My Lord," replied the queen, "You know not what love is. Before it education, cleverness, intelligence, all fly as dust does before a storm. She cannot be induced to forget love. Separation is the only remedy to cure this disease ; therefore remove the young man from her presence." The king held a council of his ministers and discussed the matter. They unanimously agreed to the proposal of the queen, but they went further and said that he ought to be killed ;—for if he be sent away who would prevent him from coming secretely to the Princess ? But was it not very cruel to kill a most innocent youngman for no fault of his ! The king really loved him ; he agreed to the foul deed only through his strong sense of duty, but he positively declined to have the deed done in his presence or when he would be in his capital. If it be done at all, it should be done as secretly as possible.

[2]

THE king and the queen with all their staff went out on a hunting-excursion. A solitary minister was left behind to administer the State and to do what he would be instructed to do by the king as regards *Chandrahásha.* The young man was ordered to accompany the royal suite, but Princess *Bishayá* was left in the capital. None knew the secret plot that was laid to remove the poor and innocent young man from this world, for not loving, but being loved by another. *Bishayá* knew nothing of it, and *Chandrahásha* never dreamt that his life had been aimed at.

The king left the capital and went to a distant forest. There he encamped and passed a few days in hunting. One day he asked *Chandrahásha* to appear before him and when he came and saluted him in due respect he addressed him thus. "I am entrusting you with a most important State paper. Take horse immediately and deliver it to the minister in charge of the State." *Chandrahásha* was greatly flattered,—his joy knew no bounds. He had been honoured with the royal confidence and had been made an agent to carry most important and confidential State papers to the royal court. He immediately took horse and rode as fast as the horse could carry him. He covered miles in minutes and flew like a whirlwind.

But his horse broke down when he had come almost at the gate of the city. The poor brute could not go a step further unless it was allowed to take some rest. *Chandrahásha* was forced to halt; he got down from his horse and sat at the foot of a tree. He was very much fatigued; as he lay half-reclined to the tree, the all-assuaging Sleep came upon him and he fell into a deep slumber.

Princess *Bishayá* was left behind in the palace and she knew not that a secret plot had been arranged to remedy the disease that had taken possession of her loving heart. She was melancholy; —she was not happy, she did not get any pleasure in any thing, but she knew not why. Is it because her parents had gone away? Is it because they were absent from her? Is it because they did not care to allow her to accompany them? No,—she was happy in her own pleasure from her childhood. Her beloved companions were all by her side; all the pleasures and luxuries were at her disposal; the whole kingdom was at her feet,—why, she had no wants to feel and no grievance to make. But she was not happy ; the fragrant flowers that were her joy, the sweet songs that were her favourites, the plays and games that were her amusements, did not and could not please her ; something was wrong somewhere. She felt a vacuum in the innermost depth of her heart and she tried not to feel it by every possible means but without any avail. *Chandrahásha* was gone and with him her joy, her pleasure, her happiness. She smiled at her own weakness, she tried to get rid of the feelings, she attempted to be merry,—but alas, all in vain ! She sang, she danced, she played, but no,—the sweet face of her lover was always before her eyes, and it made her melancholy morose and unhappy. Nothing gave her pleasure, she grew so restless ! She avoided her companions and passed hours in silent meditations. Nothing is so pleasureable as the thoughts of love. Her companions marked the change that had come upon her ; they tried all possible means to amuse her and to while away her time. They induced her to go out and play in gardens and groves ; they took her to many places, hoping to cheer her up by new scenes and new pastimes.

In one of these excursions Princess *Bishayá* came with her maids to the garden where the young man fell asleep. She tried to be happy with her companions ;

she attempted to be merry with the song and dance that were got up for her, but alas, nothing could please her. She slipped out of their company and went to the most solitary corner of the garden. There she walked alone in her own thoughts, dreaming of *Chandrahásha* and his sweet face. But was she really dreaming ! She stood amazed to find before her the very object of her love, peacefully sleeping and reclining on the trunk of a tree. She came near him and saw a packet underneath his breast-plate. What is greater than curiosity in a woman's heart ! She carefully took it up without disturbing her lover ; she opened it and read the short lines it contained. It ran as follows,—"Give without least delay *Bisha* (poison) to *Chandrahásha*, the bearer of this." The letter was signed by her own father ! Her head reeled and she would have fallen, if she did not place herself on the tree. But soon she regained her self-control and determined to save her lover. She took up a pin from her hair and with this pin and with the collyrium that was in her beautiful eyes, she carefully immitated her father's hand and added the letters *Yá* just after *Bisha* (poison). Thus it became *Bishayá* the princess, instead of *Bisha* the poison. She carefully folded the letter, placed it back where it was and left the young man to sleep quietly at the foot of the tree.

But soon *Chandrahásha* got up and hastened to the palace. He duly delivered the letter to the minister in charge. He was astonished to find that he had been ordered to bestow the royal Princess on the young man. But he thought that the king must have changed his mind and as he was accompanied by all the ministers, they must have found some strong reasons to advice him to give away the princess to *Chandrahásha*. So he made no delay; the very next morning he married the princess to *Chandrahásha* in due form and in all solemnity. What was the king's astonishment when he found on his return to the capital that the young man to whom he ordered poison to be given had become his son-in-law! He was awfully annoyed, but there was no help; it was done and could not be undone.

He reproved the minister, but he showed the king the letter in which *Bishayá* and not *Bisha* was written in very clear letters. The king thought *Chandrahásha* must have secretly opened the letter and made the alteration; but the princess appeared before her royal father, fell on her knees and said, "Father, if any body is to be punished for the act, it is I; for I did it." The king pardoned her and *Bishayá* and *Chandrahásha* became very happy.

THE DANAVA KING.

[1]

THERE rose from the ranks of the vicious and wicked *Dánava* kings a Ruler as mighty in arms, as virtuous and noble in deeds, as good, generous and charitable, as the king of the gods or the great Preserver himself. His compeers conquered the heaven and earth by their might, but king *Bali* conquered them by his goodness, by his exemplary character, by his great charity, generosity and nobleness.* *Rishis* were respected and honoured,—

* *Táraka, Betra, Shambhu,* (see Battle of Gods and demons), *Rávana,* (see the Monkey War), *Hiranyakashipu,* (see *Prahlád*) all these *Dánava* kings were powerful and great in their wickedness but here is a contrast.

learning was encouraged by endowments and grants, Brahmins were enriched and the poor were supplied with all their wants. His brother kings, his mighty predecessors,his great ancestors, conquered the lands, the cities, the kingdoms of the world and the blissful and happy sovereignty of heaven, but king *Bali* won the heart of both man and god.

Gods and Goddesses lost all hold over the heart of humanity ;—men and women began to worship king *Bali* instead of gods and goddesses. The sovereignty of heaven over the earth was gone. Well, it went further. The goodness of *Bali* rose over that of the celestial kingdom ;—gods and goddesses began to leave their happy homes and to emigrate to the blissful and loving kingdom of the *Dánava* king.

Indra, the king of the gods, lost his sovereignty over the earth and found it difficult to retain his hold over his own kingdom of heaven. He was never in such a crisis. In olden days when the *Dánavas* tried to conquer his kingdom and empire, he defended himself with arms, he gave them battle, he fought with them for years and kept them at bay at the gate of heaven,—he struggled to retain his possesions,—but here in the case of king *Bali* he could do nothing; he was thoroughly helpless. When he fought with the *Dánavas* his gods stood by him as men ; there was not a single dissentient voice, there was none who went over to the enemy's camp,—but now not one, but hundreds went over to the good and generous king *Bali.*

Indra repaired to *Baikuntha** and prayed to the great Preserver to save his Empire or to allow him to retire, so that *Bali* might be placed on the throne of heaven. "My son," said the great God, "A *Dánava* cannot be made the Ruler of heaven and earth. I shall soon go down to the world and do the needful to put you at rest."

Vishnu left his heavenly throne and took birth in the womb of *Aditi*, the wife of the great *Rishi Kashyapa*. He incarnated himself to save the sovereignty of gods over the heaven and the earth.

[2]

THE boy that was born to great *Rishi Kashyapa* was a dwarf,†—very small in stature but very intelligent in look. He appeared to be a prodigy, for he mastered the *Vedas* before he went through the ceremony of the holy-thread.‡ He was the

* *Baikuntha* is the seat of *Vishnu*.

† Dwarf was the fifth incarnation of *Vishnu*. See the note in *Prahláda*.

‡ The ceremony of holy-thread is a sort of Baptismal. It is a ceremony in which the boy begins to wear a thread round his

beloved of all the *Rishis* and the favourite of all the ladies.*

He grew up and the time for his *Braamacharya* came. *Rishi Kashyapa* solemnised the ceremony in due form and as the boy would have to maintain himself by begging alms, he was sent out to make a beginning at the palace of the most kind, generous and charitable king *Bali.*

The little man went and appeared at the court of the great *Dánava* king. None came there and went back disappointed; riches were showered over the needy in the court of king *Bali.* When the boy appeared, the king received him in great honour and asked him what he could do for him. "Oh, generous king," said the boy, "Do you promise to grant me what I shall ask from you?" "My good sir," replied the king, "I have made a vow not to refuse any body. I have never broken through the vow; therefore, you can safely ask me what you want. Know for certain that it shall be granted." "Then, Oh king," said the boy, "Give me land that

---

neck, and which, being the emblem of a Brahmin, is considered to be very holy, and enters upon his student-life. From the day of this cereomny which is called *Brahmacharya*, *i.e.* the life for preparation to be a Brahmin, he is to observe strict celebacy, to cultivate all moral virtues and to practise rigid studious habits.

* Celebacy was not the strict rule for a *Rishi.* There were many *Rishis* who were married.

would be covered by my three feet." The king and the court smiled at the boy's demand; they thought him mad; they took him for an idiot. "My good boy," said the king, "Ask riches, ask kingdom, sovereignty or whatever you will, but the small piece of land that you demand will do you no good." "No, king," replied the boy, "I want nothing else. Tell me whether you agree to give it to me or not."

The king smiled and was at the point of replying in the affirmative, when *Sukra*, the great Preceptor of the *Dánavas,* rose and said, "King, do not argee to grant the land asked for by this Brahmin boy. It will be your ruin and with you the ruin of the *Dánavas*. Know then, he is no other than great *Vishnu* himself. He has come in this shape to delude you and to take out of your hands the great sovereignty you have been able to acquire."

The king could not believe what was told to him. Who could believe that the little man before him was the great God himself! Although it was said by his great Preceptor, still he thought that the great *Rishi* could by no means be correct, at least in his this surmise.

[3]

"GREAT Preceptor," said king *Bali*, "If this boy be really *Vishnu* and has come to delude me and to take away my possessions, still I cannot but grant him what he asks, for it is the solemn vow of my life." Then he turned towards the boy and said, "My gentle sir, I agree to grant you the land you ask from me." "Oh king," replied the boy, "I thank you for your generosity. Come, bestow it on me in due form."* But where was the great Preceptor who was required to perform the ceremony of bestowal? *Rishi Sukra* had great love for king *Bali* and the *Dánava* race. He saw ruin staring the king in his face; he determined to make a last effort to save king *Bali* and the *Dánavas*. He entered into the water-pot and stopped its mouth, so that the holy-water might not fall from the pot; for it was absolutely necessary for the ceremony of bestowal.

When the Preceptor was not found, the boy told the king that he would himself perform it and officiate for his absent Preceptor. The king sat on a holy seat and tried to get water from the pot, but without avail. "Oh king," said the boy, "take one of these

* In this ceremony the bestower takes up holy water in the palm of his hands and utter some verses dictated by the Preceptor in honour of the great God.

Kusha grasses and clean the mouth of the pot." The king did as he was ordered;—he sent a *Kusha* grass through the mouth of the pot and it struck one of the eyes of the great *Rishi*, who was there to prevent the water from coming out. He was made blind and in pain and sorrow he fled from the place.

The ceremony was performed. "Oh king," said the boy, "Show me the land that you would give me." "My good boy," replied the king, "Make your own choice. I am the lord of both heaven and earth; you can select the place that you want."

At once the boy transformed himself into the mighty, unknowable, and undescribable God which he was. He covered heaven with one foot and the earth with the other. "*Bali*," said he, "I have taken earth and heaven; what else you would give me for my third foot".

The good and great *Bali* stood firm; he was unmoved; he was unchanged. "Great and mighty God," said he, "Where is your third foot that you demand land for it?" "Well," said the great Preserver, "Here it is." And a mighty leg issued from the centre of his body. "*Bali*," said *Vishnu*, "show me the land for it." "Here it is," said the king and took it on his own head. There were acclamations all over the universe and loud and continual cheerings for the great deed done by the *Dánava* king.

Well, he had given to the great God his sovereignty of heaven and earth ; well, he had given up himself too to hold his third foot,—where should he now go,—what could he now do without the command of his great Master ? He was sent to the infernal regions, there to live on refuse of men and Gods.*

* It is said that *Vishnu* gave *Bali* a chance to live in heaven. He was told that if he agreed to be accompanied by one hundred fools, he could go and live in heaven. But king *Bali* preferred living in the infernal regions to going to heaven with one hundred fools.